Classical Arab Islam

CLASSICAL ARAB ISLAM

THE CULTURE AND HERITAGE OF THE GOLDEN AGE

TARIF KHALIDI

THE DARWIN PRESS, INC.
PRINCETON, NJ 08540 USA

Library of Congress Cataloging in Publication Data

Khalidi, Tarif, 1938-
Classical Arab Islam.

Bibliography, p. 135
Includes index.
1. Civilization, Islamic. I. Title.
DS36.85.K4 1984 909′.097671 84-70416
ISBN 0-87850-047-2

Printed in the United States of America

CONTENTS

Acknowledgments

THE SUBSTANCE of this book was in origin a series of lectures on classical Islam delivered at the University of Michigan, Ann Arbor, in 1978. I have since gone back to these lectures as often as I was able, rewriting some sections and adding others, in the hope that they would serve their original introductory purpose as well as the needs of more advanced students of classical Islam.

A cluster of friendships and intellectual debts envelops a book that grows in the environment of colleagues and students. In Ann Arbor, the conversation and friendship of Professors Gernot Windfuhr, Amal Rassam, William Schorger, the late Ernest Abd al-Massih, Ernest McCarus, James Bellamy, and the late Richard Mitchell made the book possible. The detailed critical comments of Professors George Hourani and Edward Said greatly improved the first version. At the American University of Beirut, the Civilization Sequence Program and the History Department provided as always a lively forum for the discussion of the history of cultures. My colleague, Professor Lawrence Conrad, generously undertook to steer the manuscript towards publication. To them all and to almost two generations of students, my affectionate gratitude.

Finally, my family have cheerfully tolerated my frequent withdrawals from their life to work on this book, often in candle light and to the accompaniment of the booms of war. I would have dedicated this book to them had I been convinced that this would adequately discharge my debt.

Department of History
American University of Beirut
December, 1984

Tarif Khalidi

INTRODUCTION

THESE ESSAYS are primarily, though not exclusively, concerned with Arab Islamic culture of the classical period, that is, the period stretching roughly from the seventh to the thirteenth centuries A.D., when the basic cultural patterns were established, the various branches of religious and non-religious scholarship were more or less defined, and the religious life-styles had become embedded in the subconscious of an ancient ecumenical society. Islam is a commanding world culture and the thought-patterns as well as the religious life-styles established in the classical period still dominate modern Islamic consciousness, many people say suffocate it. I will be concentrating entirely on Arabic Islam, i.e., Islamic literature written in Arabic, since Arabic in the period under consideration was the principal language of Islamic culture.

In examining any world culture, a number of problems arise with which it would be best to come to grips before one prepares to launch forth. One is methodology. There is, to begin with, the debate which has recently acquired enormous intellectual vigor in the West, in part due to the work of a new breed of "angry young Orientalists." An echo of these debates in the Arab world will be found in the Conclusion (Chapter Eleven). But the problem remains: How does one present one's culture to a primarily foreign audience? By accepting, to begin with, the view that major world cultures have tended to breed very similar thought patterns. If cultures could be taken apart for closer examination, like giant computers, I suspect we would find that they have the same sort of electronic circuitry. If one cares to, one can enumerate these circuits with relative ease. Thus, I dare say that my own table of contents could, with slight modification, serve as a table of contents for an examination of Greco-Roman, Indian, Chinese, or even modern Western cultures. Readers familiar with the work of C. M. Bowra might note that "The Place of Reason" is a chapter title, or "circuit," lifted from his own classic little volume, *The Greek Experience*. Accordingly, coming to terms with any alien culture need not present the reader with insurmountable difficulties of cultural identification.

Having said this, however, one must immediately add a number of qualifers. For a Palestinian like myself, the historical examination of his own Arab Muslim culture raises, in turn, the problem of commitment. Modern Arab Muslims are locked into Islamic culture far more politically than any modern Western scholar is locked into his own medieval West. Among modern Muslims, there is a pervading sense of failure, a sense that, somehow, the classical age of Arab Islam was the Golden Age, that the Arab Islamic past was "superior" to the present. In our own day, therefore, far greater attention is being paid to reviving that culture, remolding it, whipping it into modern shape, than to studying it in a detached yet committed manner. Classical Islam, like a shuttle, repeatedly weaves itself into the very fabric of our modern thought patterns as well as our life styles, touching us at every point with its political wand. The modern Arab Muslim scholar is constantly forced to come to grips with issues that are a thousand years old or more but that still retain enormous contemporary vividness and polemicability. For this reason, Arab Islam is now in the process of an interesting overhaul and much is heard today in the Arab world about "our heritage" *(turāth)*. In fact, some modern Muslim writers have criticized Islam precisely because they think it is still too vivid and therefore has bred a non-historical spirit, where past and present are continuously being jumbled together in modern Muslim consciousness.

Accordingly, the modern Muslim scholar is frequently caught in the tormenting web of, and sometimes choice between, his or her own viable and living religious tradition on the one hand and the onslaught (intellecutal, colonialist) of the West on the other. One of the more harmful of these Western onslaughts has been the creation of a class or group of "Orientalist" Arab Muslim scholars who see Arab Islamic culture through Western eyes, who pass judgment upon it in reductionist, simplistic, or jargonistic terms, thus "aping" even the absurd generalizations of Western scholarship on Islam and Arab history.

As against the "Orientalists," there is a "chauvinist" current. This often takes the form of claiming for Arab Islamic culture a "modernity" which breathlessly tries to keep abreast of Western cultural advance, seeking to find parallels for every new theory in some early text of Arabic or Islamic culture. Between the "Oriental orientalists" and the "chauvinists," one loses sight of the civilization understood against its own historical evolution and primarily on its own terms rather than in terms of some entity opposing it or some entity that it should become. For all these reasons, the modern examination of classical Arab culture is a highly polemical subject in Arab intellectual circles today. These essays seek partially to reflect this contemporary polemical mood by calling attention to those aspects of classical Arab Islamic culture that still excite modern controversy. Thus, if the reader is surprised that no attention is paid to Arab Islamic Art, for example, this is because, quite simply, Art is not yet a *casus belli* in modern Arab Islamic cultural polemics.

These essays find their methodological consummation in the Conclusion. Without anticipating the arguments advanced therein, I shall merely adduce the following methodological insights and tips, in a rough order of priority, in order to encourage the reader, not only to read these pages, but also to criticize them.

First, it seems to me that the insights of Erik Erikson into the study of personality in a situation of conflict (see *Young Man Luther*) can profitably be harnessed in the service of the study of culture. If seen *sub specie aeternitatis*, the onslaught of the West against Arab Islam is helpful provided it forces us to examine our own cultural circuitry with greater historical exactitude. This means that the ongoing search among modern Arab Muslim thinkers for a latter-day Arab philosopher of history like Ibn Khaldūn is a healthy, indeed necessary development. For it has been argued that the vigor of historical writing in any culture is often directly proportionate to the vigor of that culture's historiographical speculation. If Ibn Khaldūn is to be of any help at all, he must continually inspire speculation about the transition from tribe-village to city life in an Arab context—even if his own models of nomadic into sedentary dynasties have fallen by the wayside. In other words, a modern reading of Ibn Khaldūn ought, among other things, to encourage us to seek for models of urban evolution as well as to shed light on the complex question of the relationship between thought patterns, power, and social class in an Arab Islamic context.

Which leads me to the second issue, namely, the relationship between classical Arab Islamic culture and the historical societies that produced it, i.e., the sociology of Islamic culture. Here, we are on far less certain ground because scholars working in the field, both Muslim and non-Muslim, have yet to produce a satisfying explanation of the culture seen against its societal background. In addition, vast areas of Islamic culture are still riddled with lacunae of ignorance.

In Turkey alone, there are tens of thousands of Arabic Islamic manuscripts that are totally unknown and uncatalogued. Works of seminal importance in classical Islamic culture are being unearthed every year, and it will take us a long time properly to digest their significance. As for the sociology of Islamic culture, anyone who attempts it has to be both a sociologist and a competent linguist, a combination that is unfortunately rather rare. So, in this particular, one must move with care. Obviously, one can no longer be a historian of ideas without also being a historian of society. So, whenever relevant, I will attempt to sketch, if only briefly and tentatively, the social and historical background of these diverse cultural thought patterns.

Thirdly, there is the question of emphasis. How does one "sample" a culture? In the centuries examined in these pages, the so-called Golden Age of Arab Islam, the volume of works on jurisprudence, or *fiqh*, was larger than that of any other branch of Islamic sciences. It was to grow even larger later on and jurisprudence quickly became the official spokesman of Arab Islamic culture. There is what Marshall Hodgson calls "moral challenge" in this culture. He argues that this moral challenge lies at the core of the classical Islamic spirit. I personally tend to shy away from words like spirit and moral challenge—but there is an unmistakeably pronounced juristic streak. However, if one were to concentrate on jurisprudence, I think one would unnecessarily circumscribe, perhaps even distort, that culture—and this for two reasons.

First, while legal works have indeed been a very large part of the total cultural production, the actual power of Islamic law (as opposed to the appeal of Islamic ideology) has tended to shrink over Muslim societies. Secondly, it is precisely the cultural diversity of a world culture that makes culture meaningful and relevant, both to believers as well as to non-believers. The law will not be ignored but the law will not dominate our interests.

Fourthly, there is the unavoidable problem of terminology in dealing with cultures from a broad historical perspective. The word "culture" is itself problematic even as it is used today in different Western academic milieux. I use it here as an outstretched translation of the Arabic word *ḥaḍāra* (note: a relatively modern, not a classical word) to mean primarily thought pattern plus lifestyle.

What word did classical Arab Islam use for this? One of the nearest, perhaps, is *Āthār*, meaning the vestiges, remains, or heritage, material and intellectual, of past ages. To a classical scholar, it denoted the legacy of ancient nations, since he did not feel he had much to learn from contemporaneous nations. Classical Islam believed that it had inherited not only a pristine religion but also a pristine wisdom, composed of the arts, sciences, and crafts of earlier nations. In this way, classical Islam defined itself and its wisdom vis-à-vis the past, and thought of itself as, in a real sense, a continuator of earlier civilizations.

It remains for me to call attention to two stylistic points. First, I have not endeavored to change the tone of these essays, preferrring them, on the whole, to be read as lectures rather than as chapters in a book. The disadvantage, hopefully reduced to a minimum, is that lectures tend to be repetitive in places and to accommodate themselves to peculiarities of time, place, and audience. The advantage, however, is that even repetition may serve to reinforce what is often difficult and culturally "alien" argumentation. Additionally, this tone might also preserve some of the freshness of the original delivery and may therefore be found more vivid. Second, the transliteration from the Arabic has generally followed a simplified version of the system adopted by the *Encyclopedia of Islam*, except where certain terms and place-names would be more familiar to the reader in their common English form.

Chapter One

THE FOUNDATIONS

FOR THE MUSLIM, as for the Christian or Jew, his religion is not one of a number of competing religions, but the final and ultimate religion, the quintessence of revelation, the ecumenical faith. Furthermore, Islam is not a new religion but rather the renewal or revival of an eternal monotheism which was born with the world. Among other things, this has meant, as I have already indicated in the Introduction, an intense Islamic consciousness of history, an obsession with history. You will see this when you read even briefly in the Koran. There you will see a panorama of history unfolding, complete with Old Testament and New Testament prophets, where you will find Abraham, Moses, Jacob, Mary, and Jesus all speaking and behaving like Muslims. This panorama begins with Islam and ends with Islam, begins with Adam and ends with Muḥammad, who is the restorer rather than the innovator. All truly pious and righteous men of the past, present, and future are by definition Muslim—a theme I shall be returning to later.

We know quite a lot about the origin and development of Islam, more than we know about the early origins and development of Christianity. We know a great deal about its founder, Muḥammad, about his life, his mission, and how the religion spread. Therefore, I will simply concentrate on certain topics which seem interesting to me and on which I have myself done some reflection or writing.

One must, of course, begin with the Koran, which we shall later be examining in more detail, and which has been the single most influential religious, literary, linguistic, theological, and legal product of Islamic culture. For Muslims, it is not a book about religion or God but rather it is God's book—the direct revelation of the speech of God revealed to His Prophet Muḥammad over a number of years and on different occasions through the mediation of the angel Gabriel. The speaker is at all times God Himself, never Muḥammad. It is God who has chosen to restore the human community to the True

Path. Only God can see where the story of mankind began and where it will all end.

There is in the Koran a sense of awesome finality. Why awesome? Because the immediacy of this Divine revelation is as blinding to man as is lightning and as deafening as thunder (I am not being poetical—these images are in the Koran and are repeated again and again). God, so to speak, has taken over the human condition; God has overpowered the world; God is the only Guardian of humanity; and the Koran is God's ultimate proof, sign and guidance, Muḥammad's crowning miracle. It is as if God finally decided to intervene in this mass of squabbling humanity and once and for all has put an end to the ceaseless and useless polemics of the diverse religious communities. Echoes of these polemics are found frequently in the Koran. A powerful image here is the Great Cry, the Great Scream of God that will signal the end of the world, and put an end to all the blabbering of humanity, all the violent debates that have wracked and torn the human community: "They can expect only the Great Cry, which will overwhelm them as they dispute" (Koran 36:49). There is a tremendous cosmic drama being enacted here and those unbelievers who do not hear or perceive it, who reject the immediacy of the message, are often referred to as self-deceivers or hypocrites. Hell and Heaven are a present dimension. Those who dispute and argue and challenge the Divine reality are in hell already. The Islamic Hell, like the Hell of Dante, is the place of discord, *par excellence*.

In place of discord and dispute, the Koran puts forth the ideal of a Muslim community *(umma)*, one of whose essential attributes is to act as an arbiter, a compromise community, a middle group, a synthesis one might say, a settler of religious arguments. The Islamic community is described as the witnesses of God on earth. They always will perform this function of social cohesion, replacing the ceaseless and useless polemics of Christians and Jews and their intense sectarianism with the simple and straightforward recognition of the Divine Reality. On the individual psychological level, the contrast is between the disputing and divided soul on the one hand and the soul at peace with God on the other, the discordant soul and the harmonious soul, between the many gods created by men and the One God who dominates the human situation. The true believers, therefore, are often spoken of as "brothers," souls that are at peace with themselves and with each other and bound together by a faith that gives them the wisdom to see what must be obvious to anyone with any sincerity of insight. In this awesome presence of God, in this cosmic drama, even Muḥammad, the last and greatest of the prophets, occupies a back seat. In the Koran, he is a man who lays no claims to wealth, divination, or sanctity. He merely follows what is revealed to him. He disclaims any role of guardianship, since guardianship belongs solely to God. In Chapter 7, verse 188, for example, he admits his weakness and inability to bring about good or evil. As a diviner or fortune teller, he could have amassed riches but he knows nothing of the future, and is just a man chosen by God to warn men of faith. In Chapter 26, verse 127, the phrase, "I ask of you no wages for this: my wage falls only upon the Lord of the Worlds," is one that is often repeated, not just by Muḥammad, but also by other Koranic prophets. It is meant to distinguish prophets in general from seers or fortune tellers who charge money for their pronouncements. The true prophet gives his warnings free of charge.

But the awesome or fearful aspect of God is only one aspect, because the terror of God's presence, the fear aroused, is then meant to soften the hearts to God. (This imagery you will find in Chapter 39.) This is almost like the definition of tragedy by Aristotle: pity or fear followed by reconciliation and purgation. The way towards reconciliation with God, therefore, lies through self-mortification, purifying the soul from all other concerns except the quest for God. This quest must be undertaken with patience. Be patient, or better still, be steadfast in the worship of God, is a recurrent admonition in the Koran. "Draw close to God"; "Draw near"; "Make the Lord your quest"—these are all very frequent admonitions especially in the short Meccan chapters. And this is because the horizons of this world are filled with the justice of God.

Second in importance to the Koran in Islam are the Traditions or *Ḥadīth* of the Prophet. When the Prophet died in A.D. 632, his prestige was still to come. The fabulously successful wars of conquest and the rapid establishment of a vast Arab Muslim empire served only to enhance his standing and achievements, and success was taken to be a triumphant proof of the truth of his mission. Almost overnight, Islam became the religion of an empire, and its founder was endowed with super-human attributes. Every word he ever uttered, every action he did was taken to be exemplary. Now social life was becoming more intricate; there were economic upheavals on an enormous scale; and there were problems of administration and taxation and conversion to which the new Muslim empire needed urgent answers. Here the laws of the Koran had to be supplemented by the practice of the Prophet. Within 200 years after his death, millions of these "traditions" were in circulation. And when these traditions came to be codified in the ninth century A.D., they were accepted by the community as having a binding religious legality. However, many were also recognized as being of shaky historical authenticity. But the legal scholars of that period were not primarily concerned with this problem of authenticity. They evolved rough and ready criteria for testing the historical truth of these reports, one of the most common ways being to question the veracity of the transmitters of each report. What these legal scholars had in mind was the overall interest of the community (if you are a Marxist, you would, of course, say the overall interest of their class). Such reports of the Prophet, which purportedly encouraged customs, manners, and habits clearly beneficial to the community, were accepted even if their authenticity was questionable. The *Ḥadīth*, or Traditions, have had a very important sociological significance in the history of Islam. Within this corpus of traditions supposedly dating back to the Prophet have been incorporated the manners and customs of diverse nations who embraced Islam. Hence, the *Ḥadīth* has had the effect of broadening the appeal of Islam to many different kinds of societies. It acted as a catalyst, drawing into the faith wider and wider circles of humanity. The most intense theological, legal, economic, and administrative viewpoints strove to gain respectability by becoming traditions from the Prophet. They are, as you might imagine, often contradictory. Let me give you an example. "So and so related to me on the authority of so and so that the Prophet said, 'Trade is the most honorable occupation.' " "So and so related to me that the Prophet said, 'Trade is the most dishonorable occupation and the dishonest merchant is in hell already.' " The topic is wide open for dispute but—and this is very important—the dispute takes place within the same framework; it takes place within the faith, not outside it. Islamic legal theory, therefore, has always accommodated itself to new situations with relative ease.

But every religion, however accommodating, develops certain internal restrictions on its own central dogmas exercised very frequently by groups who devote their lives to its study. In early Christianity, this was excerised by the church councils, which met to determine what church doctrine was on any particular issue. In Islam, the mechanism was much less formal than that of a church council but no less real. It took the form of the consensus of the learned men of each generation *(ijmā*ᶜ*)* and that consensus was carried forward by each succeeding generation. Now this may sound very vague. Who is to determine what the consensus is? How is a consensus achieved anyway? These are all very difficult questions, but Islam ultimately managed to survive these problems. True, these problems split the community into two halves, Sunnī Islam and Shīᶜī Islam, and the history of their relationship has not always been a happy one. There were periods when they coexisted peacefully; others when they fought each other violently. But the quarrel did not sap the vitality of the faith. In the twentieth century, the quarrel, at least over theory, has been reduced to the dimensions of minor ritualistic practices.

But to return briefly to consensus, which ranks third in importance to the Koran and Traditions as a source of dogma and law. The most plausible explanation of how consensus was achieved is perhaps the sociological one. These scholars of law tended to belong to certain social classes, usually traders or artisans, whose common opinions may well have been influenced by their common mode of life. Their opinions and values reflected themselves in a certain uniformity of interpretation of sacred texts, in the recognition of common interpretations as binding. Being often the most influential members of their community, they were able to enforce their views.

The fourth source of Islamic dogma and law is argument or reasoning by analogy *(qiyās)*. In other words, it is the manner in which legal scholars derive a particular commandment or prohibition from a general commandment or prohibition. If wine is prohibited, for example, so is whiskey or beer because it is the alcohol rather than the particular drink which is prohibited. Charity is commanded to relatives and friends. So, by analogy, is charity to charitable institutions.

Islam, therefore, spreads its message at four different levels: the Divine, the Prophetic, the Communal, and the Individual. Islam as revealed by God is in the Koran; as taught by the Prophet it is in *Ḥadīth*; as interpreted by the scholarly community it is in the consensus; as refined by the individual it is in analogical reasoning. The Divine, the prophetic, the communal, the individual: in that order of importance.

Now the possession by the Muslims of a sacred text—which is the very word of God, where every letter, every word, every phrase has a divine character—disposed the Muslims from the earliest times to develop and refine the disciplines of philology and law, considered essential for the proper understanding of the Koranic text. As *Ḥadīth* developed rapidly, it in turn begat the disciplines of history and biography, these disciplines again considered essential for filling in the gaps, as it were, in the accounts of the Koran and the Traditions. Philology and law, history and biography, were among the earliest Muslim religious sciences. In all these fields, the Muslims made very important contributions, not to mention the equally important contributions in theology and natural science. But all these sciences continued to be written under the aegis of the Koran. The scientist calculating his astronomical tables no less than the theologian or the historian would feel impelled to begin his work with a preface in which he attempted to show how his particular field of knowledge was commanded or encouraged by the Koran. Far from stultifying Islamic culture, the Koran on the contrary seemd to have inspired it.

Let me end these remarks on the dogmatic foundations of Islam by saying something about the chief sects of Islam. Max Weber has argued that a religion of salvation, such as Islam, often changes its nature when it casts its net over wider and wider social groups. In other words, it is understood differently by different classes and groups. In an urban intellectualist environment, a religion may well assume quite a different form from that which it assumes in the countryside. So far, this seems self-evident. What is perhaps less self-evident is the fact that when religion reaches the less privileged social classes, it is often transformed in the direction of a more personalized relationship, the emergence of a semidivine or divine personage who is an essential intermediary for salvation. This often takes the form of a cult of saints, a form of worship which is well-known in all religions except perhaps Judaism and Protestantism.

Islam, too, underwent the same process. In the prosperous cities of the Muslim empire and particularly among the wealthy merchant classes or craftsmen, we have the development of what later became Sunnī Islam: an Islam that was legalistic in spirit, politically quietist, i.e., tending to support the powers that be and emphasizing the unity of the community above all other socioethical values, rationalist and literal in its interpretation of texts, on the whole tolerant, emphasizing the inward nature of faith, and emphasizing faith at the expense of works. Sunnī Islam is the Islam of the great cities: of Cairo, Damascus, Baghdad, Jerusalen, Tunis, Fez, and Marrakesh. Sunnī Islam is often called Orthodox Islam, wrongly, I think, because the word "orthodox" has often stood for a value-judgment rather than a dogmatic mainstream. But the other great wing of Islam, Shīʿī

Islam, must also be briefly described to round out this discussion. In origin, Shīᶜī Islam began as a political party based on the belief that political authority should reside in the family of the Prophet, particularly in ᶜAlī,* son-in-law and cousin of Muḥammad. When the party of ᶜAlī was defeated politically in 661, it became a religious sect that regarded ᶜAlī and his descendants as guardians of the faith, infallible expositors whose pronouncements on doctrine were binding. For Shīᶜī Islam, therefore, ᶜAlī and his 11 descendants, are the intermediaries between God and men. They are not prophets, they do not bring new revelation because that would be anti-Islamic—Muḥammad being the last Prophet—but rather infallible teachers of religion. In Shīᶜī Islam one finds a more personal, dynamic relationship between man and God, more so than in the somewhat austere legalistic framework of Sunnī Islam. Early Shīᶜism was generally militant, emphasizing the importance of the ruler's integrity, whose only guarantee is Prophetic lineage. The great love and devotion expressed by the Shīᶜīs for ᶜAlī and his 11 descendants enriched Islamic thought immensely in areas like mysticism and theology. In formal terms, however, there is very little that distinguishes Sunnī from Shīᶜī Muslims today. The Shīᶜīs, for example, have somewhat more liberal inheritance laws and have minor differences in worship and so forth. However, it is noticeable that many of the earliest and most enthusiastic supporters of Shīᶜī Islam were less privileged social classes of the towns and the peasantry of the countryside. But we are still not at a point where we can reach definite conclusions on this topic.

In sum, Islam claims manifest linguistic intelligibility and puts itself forward as the religion of instinct and clarity. A priesthood is therefore excluded, not only because the Koran itself condemns the material corruption to which priesthood is prone but also because, in the Koran, mankind has finally encountered the Word of God.

Chapter Two

GOD AND HIS MESSAGE

IN INTRODUCING THE Koran, I shall talk about four major themes. The first is the historical setting or background, i.e., the society that is described in the Koran. The second is the doctrinal content of the Koran, i.e., its theology. The third is the narrative content in the Koran, i.e., the stories or narratives of prophets and kings, which, in my view, have spiritual, psychological, historical, and legal implications. The fourth and final theme is the divine magic of the Koran, its mysterious or miraculous nature and the peculiar Sufi or mystic interpretation of the Koran.

First, then, the historical setting. Mecca on the eve of Islam in the late sixth century A.D. was a peripheral city of the Hellenistic world of a type which one might describe as a commercial oligarchy. It was ruled basically by half a dozen leading merchant families who organized a caravan trade running north-south and acted as investors and bankers for most of the city people. The loss of a single caravan could mean losses for a large part of the population, whereas most of the profit made was collected by the ruling merchant elite. Because of their wealth, this elite was of course politically very powerful and ran the affairs of the city and its few institutions.

The Mecca of Muḥammad's days was a new city but an old foundation. It had only recently been taken over by the alleged ancestor of the tribe of Muḥammad, the tribe of Quraysh—whether fact or fiction is immaterial—but this tribal takeover was still in Muḥammad's days very much a living and influential memory. It was new in the sense that a tribal mentality had not yet given way to civic feeling. It was new in the economic sense also: its hardwon prosperity, no doubt assured through economic skills acquired as guardians of an old sanctuary, stood to increase even more as its geographical location began to become more and more important, as I shall show later on.

It had not, however, shed the poverty of its poorer citizens, who continued to occupy the suburbs of the city and to resent the nouveaux riches of the city center. It must, therefore, have been a city of vivid contrasts: poor and rich; merchant-aristocrat and commoner; newly-acquired urban ways and customs on the one hand and older, more communal tribal virtues on the other; urban sophistication vs. tribal simplicity. You will find echoes of all this in the Koran.

The political nexus of the city was a Council of Elders made up of the leading members of this merchant oligarchy. Their new and increasing prosperity had given them poise, self-confidence, and arrogance, which you will also observe to be reflected in the Koran. These men had shrewdly and painstakingly forged a network of alliances and contacts, essential for their caravan trade, and had cleverly abstained from involvement in the international politics of their day. They had probably learnt the lesson of their Arab neighbors and kinsmen, the Arab border kingdoms that had acted as agents of the two superpowers of their day: the Byzantine empire and the Persian empire. By the time Muḥammad was born, roughly in 570, these Arab border states had been destroyed by their imperial masters and the Meccan aristocrats wisely decided to remain neutral, to benefit from the new opportunities.

It is very important for us to understand the social setting of the Koran, i.e., this Meccan society in which Muḥammad grew up and against which he ultimately revolted. And here it would seem to me essential to make use of the insights furnished by modern disciplines like anthropology and sociology. This, as I have already indicated, is only just beginning to take place in Islamic studies, and so I offer my own analysis as tentative rather than final.

Paraphrasing the words of Georges Balandier, we might describe Meccan society as one where government and political life were diffused, where politics depended upon relationships between individuals and clans, i.e., was not based on specific institutions but on various dynamisms: competition and domination, coalition and opposition. In societies of this kind, the political sphere is reduced to a minimum. Nevertheless, they still retain their characteristics as a dynamic system. The most influential men were characterized by their clan position (i.e., aristocrats), by their lineal position as heads of extended families, by their age group (i.e., they enjoyed the status of elders), by their wealth, and by their "strong personalities." In the absence of a well differentiated political authority, power, prestige, and influence were the result of a combination of these inequalities. Justice was carried out through arbitration of disputes, often done by members of clans outside the dominant clan groups, often by members of priestly clans. Thus, Muḥammad is said to have acted as an arbitrator before he received revelation and is said to have been called *al-amīn* (the trustworthy). This fits in neatly with what we know of similar societies where second-class clans act as arbitrators for the aristocrats.

Commercial malpractices (e.g., Koran 2:282-286) were a frequent cause of grievance, and they were usually dealt with through collective action or alliances. It was felt that growing wealth made the merchant aristocrats indifferent to the sufferings of the poorer classes, and their luxury was all the more glaring because of the austere conditions of life in Arabia (e.g., 17:31). Thus, clans of the second order of importance would occasionally band together to prevent the arbitrary malpractice of the top-ranking clans. The injustices and the emphasis placed on wealth by the top clans undoubtedly impressed itself on the Prophet's personality and is so obviously reflected in the Koran. Several scholars have pointed out how much the vocabulary of the Koran is filled with commercial and mercantilist ideas. The Last Day, for example, is a day when there is no "selling or spending" (2:254). Nothing could impress the Meccans more as an image to represent the end of all activity. God is a sort of keeper of accounts who records each man's debts and credits. He "settles accounts quickly" (5:4). Another dominant image is the image of balance, where man's actions are weighed. In addition to all this, there is a distinct note of hostility in the Koran against hoarding of money as practiced, e.g., by Christians and Jews, as well as others who hoard gold and silver and do not spend it in the cause of God (9:34). (This, incidentally, had important consequences in early Arab Islamic history because when the great wave of conquests began, the early caliphs deliberately and consistently circulated the money of the Near East, which had been hoarded by the imperial treasuries of Persia and Byzantium.)

The type of society against which Muḥammad was to revolt was therefore self-satisfied, commercially minded, conservative in its mood, careful not to rock the boat, so to speak, either politically or religiously, justifying its existence by reference to a supposedly hallowed past, with a haughty aristocratic leadership jealously guarding its privileges by appealing to the "ways of our ancestors." In fact, one of the earliest objections to Muḥammad is that he is changing these ancient ways—a very telling objection to his message in a society where, in the absence of institutions and laws, precedent was all-important. Against this conservatism, the Koranic outburst at 37: 69-71 proclaims: "They found their fathers erring, and they run in their footsteps. Before them erred most of the ancients."

The social and economic tension was reflected in a religious tension, or perhaps increased and intensified an already existing religious tension. Christian and Jewish ideas were well known to the Meccans, since many Arabian tribes had converted already to either Christianity or Judaism. In the sixth century, the Yemen was the scene of a bloody war between Christians and Jews, supported and exploited by the two superpowers of the day. Meccan merchants, travelling either north into Syria and Egypt or south into the Yemen could easily become acquainted with Christianity or Judaism—and often did—but the Meccans preferred to remain neutral because religious affiliation also signified political affiliation to an imperial power. Nevertheless, one can speak of a monotheistic climate in Arabia in which even the word Allah (God) was known and in which, according to Muslim belief, there always existed individuals who, in every past age, had preserved the pure monotheistic faith that was ultimately revealed as Islam. The word, *ḥanīf*, is often translated as "pure of faith" and is, significantly, applied most of all to Abraham: the prototype of the true believer in the Koran. Abraham, therefore, is the first Muslim (2:124-143).

Muḥammad himself belonged to the clan Hāshim. In the Prophet's days, the clan had fallen into the second rank in political and economic importance. In other words, they were not members of the ruling elite. When Muḥammad was a young man, his clan banded together with other, second-class clans, to check the dictatorial behavior of the ruling clans. In fact, according to the Koran, the ruling elite has *always* been the bitterest enemies of prophets: the Koran calls this elite the Council *(al-mala')*. (The word is mentioned several times in Chapter 7 in connection with various prophets.) They are also called the "proud Council." Some modern historians and sociologists have argued that prophets have often, historically speaking, belonged to second-class clans or social groups. From this intermediate social position, prophets were able to observe their society with particular acuteness and objectivity.

When Muḥammad first began to receive revelation, around the year 610, he was already about forty years old, a man of moderate wealth and well respected in his city. But he was not a member of the city's ruling group. Almost the first objections he had to face when he announced his mission were the objections of the Meccan snobs. "Why you?" they would ask. "What is so special about you? If God had wanted to send a prophet to Mecca, he would surely have chosen one of a dozen or so Meccan aristocrats, eminently suitable men who would do the job more effectively" (a paraphrase of *Ḥadīth*). The scorn with which his preaching was received was unmistakeable and is frequently reflected in the Koran. This scorn was directed both against him personally (e.g., Koran 25:7 and 8—"What ails this Messenger that he eats food and goes in the markets?" "You are only following a man bewitched," which is answered in 25:20—"And we sent not before thee any Envoys but that they ate food and went in the markets") as well as against his preaching, where the most frequent objection was against his preaching of the physical resurrection of the body (e.g., Koran 34:7—roughly translated: "Come and hear this fellow who says you will be put together again after you have been torn to shreds!").

When Muḥammad was finally forced to emigrate from Mecca to Medina* in 622, the year which marks the beginning of the Muslim Calendar, this was not so much an act of emigration as an act of abandonment *(hijra)*. This abandonment of the sinful city also created a lingering suspicion of all cities and of city life, but this is a wider and more complex topic. Muḥammad abandoned Mecca and then proceeded to organize its ultimate conquest from his new base in Medina. Islam has been described as a "Tale of Two Cities," which I take to mean the city that rejected God and His Prophet and the city that accommodated him and allowed him to organize the earliest Muslim community, or *umma*.

To return to the Koran. The Koran, as I have already pointed out, was revealed to Muḥammad over a span of some twenty years and on different occasions through the mediation of the angel Gabriel. It is, to repeat, the speech of God; hence, in Arabic it is called simply "The Book" *(al-kitāb)*. It is a miracle of God, the greatest of all His miracles. It is essential to bear in mind this distinction between the Koran and the Old and New Testaments. To the Muslim, God is as near to you as any physical copy of the Koran.

Let me therefore introduce my second theme, which is the doctrinal content of the Koran, by saying that its theology is timeless. It faces backward to the beginning of the world and forward to its end. The Koran is the final revelation of an eternal religion which all prophets have been preaching from the beginning of the world (Koran 4:163). To restore, and by restoring, to reform—this is the doctrinal thrust of the Koran. This is what all earlier prophets have tried to do. And this is why all earlier prophets have in fact been Muslim.

This sense of the eternity of the message is the cause of what one might describe as the impersonality or anonymity of that message: "Prophets we've told you of, prophets not"—4:164. It underlies the eternal universality of the appeal of Koranic doctrine. The most vivid story, in this context, is perhaps the story of the Sleepers in the Cave (Koran 18:9), a group of believers who take shelter in a cave because they want to escape the disbelief of their community. Time passes them by until God finally decides to bring them forth again to bear witness to the true and eternal faith. Here is a story well known to Muḥammad's society from Christian or Jewish sources. In the Koran, however, their story is told like a journey in a time machine, the journey of men of pure faith moving backward and forward in time, a vivid illustration of the timeless theology of the Koran.

What sort of God does one meet in the Koran? He is, to begin with, unlike anything that human reason can imagine. There is no God but He, no reality as real as He. When a man recognizes this reality of God, he is overwhelmed, terrified, overshadowed. It is a moment that frequently catches man unprepared, hiding away from this frightening encounter. This awful moment came to Muḥammad frequently in his early Meccan days. In Chapter 74, said to be among the very earliest revelations, Muḥammad is spoken to as "enwrapped in thy robes." The moment of recognition is a moment of unveiling these robes, taking the robes off to reveal the reality of God beyond: from the "darkness" of ignorance to the "light" of recognition. The Koran continues (73:8): "And remember the name of thy Lord and devote thyself to Him very devoutly." In other words, once this reality is recognized, it must be kept steadfastly in view. Once again, the importance of constancy to God. This act of recognition is called *ḥikma* or wisdom, thought, reflection (Koran 2:269), an essential ingredient of faith (cf. St. Paul).

Exploring further this and other similar passages of the Koran, we see how near God is to His creation and how immediate is His response to man. Heaven and hell are both within the easy reach of man. The responsibility laid upon man's shoulders is very heavy—like a bird tied around his neck is what the Koran says (17:13). The imagery of night and day, dawn and twilight, forenoon and brooding darkness, illustrate repeatedly the awesome presence or absence of God. Whether you see God or whether you don't, He is still there in reality (24:39). This nearness of God is further reflected in the formula that serves as an opening to every chapter in the Koran: "In the name of God, the Merciful, the Compassionate," where the two words in Arabic, *Raḥmān* and *Raḥīm*, stand respectively for God as mercy *(Raḥmān)* with a capital M and God as compassionate *(Raḥīm)*, actively involved in creation, "nearer to man than his jugular vein." God is both the principle of Mercy as well as the merciful: transcendent and immanent as the theologians might put it.

God is also the One, an image which is predominant in the Koran. The one God can have nothing besides Him. This for the Muslim remains the single most important attribute of God (112:1). All sins are in theory forgivable except the terrible sin of polytheism *(shirk)*, that is, ascribing partners to God (4:48, 116). To believe in many gods is really to deny reason, to upset the natural order of the world. Polytheism is not only theologically irrational; it also engenders political chaos, schism, discord (21:22; 23:91). Hence, to uphold God's unity is also to uphold the political unity of mankind—using the word "political" here in its widest sense.

All things shall "come home" to God (24:42). Therefore, all things manifest and proclaim His presence. The Koran repeatedly urges man to look around him, to contemplate the world, to deduce from the passing phenomena of the world, of nature and of history, the active presence and the hand of God. The world is full of the "signs" of God *(Āyāt)*. From the design, one must deduce the designer. As in Jeremiah, the pot proves the existence of the potter, so in the Koran the whole world proves the existence of its maker (56:63). To those who remain obstinate in their ignorance, enwrapped in their cloaks, self-centered, God reveals Himself as the Avenger, causing the earth and sky to tremble, the mountains to shake, Lord of the Day of Judgment, the Elevator and the Destroyer.

This in brief is the God of the early chapters of the Koran. Many of these teachings are directed against Mecca, more often implicitly than explicitly. What is being condemned here is the city of men, a society of sophisticated and ruthless merchants, spiritually indifferent to God (36:46). But the language remains impersonal and nonspecific. It is not just Mecca that is being condemned but a certain type of human society often associated with the city (e.g., 4:75). In fact, as I have already suggested, the Koranic attitude to the city remains ambivalent. For while the city is the only locus of prophecy, it is also prone to diseases like luxury, corrupt mercantile practices, dictatorial kings, proud and rebellious spirits of all kinds who refuse to recognize the God in their midst. Paradise, therefore, is not a "city" of God, as you might find it in the Roman Christian view. The Muslim paradise is not a perfect city or city-state. Rather, it is the garden of God; it is man living in a perfected nature.

From this I would like to pass on to my third theme, namely the narrative content of the Koran together with what I feel to be its spiritual, psychological, and legal implications. This narrative part of the Koran forms, relatively speaking, a considerable portion of the whole. It is made up of stories of ancient kings and prophets, frequently interrupting the narrative to point to the moral of the story in question, which is the activity of God in history. The significance is perfectly clear: God is not only here and now but has always been there and then. He has created kingdoms and cities, often more powerful than now: "Yet look at their end" (30:9). Many of these stories are supposedly familiar to the audience since they are so often introduced as reminders ("Have you not seen?" "Have you not heard?"). The Koran, therefore, does not narrate so much as illustrate the deeper and inward significance of these stories. This moral is summed up in the single, very meaningful Arabic word *ᶜibra*, which has had a long history in Islamic culture, culminating in Ibn Khaldūn. The word comes from the root verb *ᶜabara*, meaning to cross over or to pass beyond. Hence, in the Koran, one is meant to "cross over" from the outward story to its inner significance or true meaning. The Koran, therefore, is a deeply historical work, although not a history book. It seeks to remind man of the presence of God in history, a presence which has always expressed itself in terms of a religion called Islam, brought to the world by a succession of prophets who, in essence, repeat the historical experience of Muḥammad himself. Not only is this true of the Biblical prophets like Abraham, Moses, and Jacob. It is even more true of these mysterious Arabian prophets: Hūd, Ṣāliḥ, Shuᶜaib, who have often puzzled Koranic scholars and who, to my mind, are really psychological *alter egos* of Muḥammad himself.

The Koranic "philosophy of history," if one wishes to call it so, has as its main theme the struggle throughout history between the righteous and the unrighteous, good men and evil men, prophets and kings. (This theme is to be found in later Arabic Islamic historical writing, which I shall discuss further on; thus, Ṭabarī* [tenth century], perhaps the greatest of the early Muslim historians, entitled his work *The History of Prophets and Kings,* clearly an echo of the Koranic view of history.) It is in their constant struggle that we perceive the deepest cause for the rise and fall of states, kingdoms, and nations. At the heart of this historical drama is the Koranic word *fitna*, the most prominent social evil. *Fitna* means many things. It means, among others, "temptation," "seduction," "trial," "civic discord." It is meant to suggest the view that catastrophe always falls upon the unprepared, the self-deceived, those who have been tempted by the world to deviate from the path of true recognition and so end up by destroying themselves. This temptation often takes the form of material luxury which, when it reaches its height, produces spiritual corruption, and God intervenes with terrible swiftness (e.g., 41:16, 17). On the individual or psychological level, it takes the form of religious sects who divide religion, each sect being satisfied with what they have (e.g., 30:32). Here, one must of course keep in mind the historical setting. Arabia since early Christian times was known to be a favorite refuge of sects and heresies escaping from the persecution of imperial religions—just as many mountain or desert regions in the Near East have, historically speaking, bred heresies or accommodated heretics fleeing from the established religions of the great cities. "Ex Arabia semper aliquid novi" is how the Romans put it: "From Arabia always something new." When Islam burst out of Arabia, it was only natural for its enemies to think of it as yet another heresy: a belief that you will still find occasionally even today among certain Orientalists who argue that Islam is merely a Christian heresy. In other words, it was accused of being precisely what the Koran says it is not: a heresy.

This philosophy of history also takes into account the lives and sufferings of earlier prophets, many of whom I have already described as Muḥammad's *alter egos*. Men refuse to take notice of their warnings because they see them as mortals, like themselves, and thus cannot see why mere mortals can have access to a higher reality than the rest of us (e.g., 9:124). No prophet has been completely successful because no prophet has ever completely succeeded in making men look beyond the realm of the human, in making men transcend their human condition. This is why so many prophets have been sent in the past and why the moment has finally come when God Himself is to intervene and to declare the final truth. The Koran, therefore, is the "best of discourses," "the Book with the truth" (39:2, 23), the discourse to end all discourse, you might say.

This does not mean that human history is about to end, as, for example, you may find in the Gospel of Mark and in much of early Christian literature. The Koran does not proclaim the imminent end of the world, but it does proclaim the end of Prophecy. Why? Simply because, with the Koran, we have God's ultimate message. God has finally become first person singular. No wonder, therefore, that the literalist interpretation of the Koran has always had a powerful following in Islamic history.

So much for the Koranic God. The next question might be, what about Koranic man? What sort of life does man lead according to the Koran? The main features of that life are its preoccupation with amusements, with shallow ostentation, with frivolities. Koranic man is essentially fickle, easily distracted into old habits of mind and action, indifferent to the after-life (e.g., 4:137, 17:11). Against this, the Koran enjoins constancy to God. The grandeur of this conception is that the Koran here instructs both Muḥammad *and* his community. Muḥammad, so to speak, stands and listens *with* his community. In one passage of the Koran, Muḥammad is rebuked by God for a burst of hasty anger (Chapter 80). But Muḥammad grows in constancy to this Lord, and constancy to God is the backbone of faith. When the later mystics or Sufis of Islam examined this concept in the Koran, they compared constancy to God to a faithful lover, who loves his beloved for purely selfless motives, love not born in greed or lust or fear but true and selfless devotion. Several Islamic anthologies include that beautiful story of the famous woman mystic of Baghdad, Rābiʿah al ʿAdawiyya, who was seen walking the streets of Baghdad with a bucket of water in one hand and a flaming torch in the other. When asked why she was doing this, she said (and I paraphrase): "I want to burn heaven down with the torch and quench the fires of hell with the water, so that mankind would come to love God selflessly, neither out of greed for paradise, nor out of fear of hell." In the Koran the moral is clear: man is fickle and inconstant, loving God at one moment, forsaking Him the next.

Man in the Koran, like man in Christian theology, has both an actual and a symbolic dimension. He is not only a man, he is also a moral model, *ʿibra*. He is not only created; he is created for a purpose. "Surely we guided him upon the way, whether he be thankful or unthankful" (76:3). Is he free or is he predestined? This is a perennial theological problem of both Christianity and Islam. From the semantic point of view, the debate itself may be meaningless, but the fact that the debate probably began even in Muḥammad's day makes it historically important even if it is logically insoluble. Islam was born in an atmosphere that was already highly charged from the theological point of view. In contrast to both Christianity and Judaism, where there is a considerable time span between the sacred text and the appearance of systematic theology, this time lag was much shorter for Islam. Among other things, it has meant that the Koran is far more abstract than other sacred books, and despite the allusions to contemporary incidents, there is a conscious attempt made to keep these allusions vague and indirect. So, to return to free will and predestination, we find quite clearly in the Koran that God plays an active role in the human drama (e.g., 9:14, 25, 26). The troops of God, who are the angels, fight alongside the Muslims. With such a powerful and all-knowing God, man's freedom becomes a relative although a real problem.

These stories of prophets and kings are meant to be factually true but at the same time are allegories of the human soul. To read and understand the lives of Abraham, Moses, Jesus, and Mary, and finally Muḥammad, is to grasp the relevance and significance of their lives for your own, to relive, internalize, and to experience once more their experiences. The Koran asks: "Have you not heard?" "Have you forgotten these tales?" It is filled with questions whose purpose is to turn man from a condition of doubt to a condition of certainty (53:28). The true believer possesses certainty *(yaqīn)*, the non-believer can only possess doubt or conjecture *(ẓann)*. This constant urging in the Koran to look to history or to look to nature came to occupy a prominent place in Muslim learning, as I have already indicated. The Muslim sciences of all kinds were grounded in this Koranic injunction to contemplate the world. Historians, philosophers, scientists, mystics always justified what they were doing to their contemporaries, many of whom were suspicious of their activities, on the grounds of the Koran's commandments to investigate man and nature.

Muḥammad in Mecca was a persecuted preacher. Muḥammad in Medina was first an arbitrator, finally a ruler of a powerful Muslim community that had conquered roughly half of Arabia by the time of the Prophet's death in 632. The Koran reflects this social and political activity by including a certain amount of legislation, which forms the basis of Muslim law, political theory, and constitutional thought. There has been some argument about the legal portions of the Koran in recent years. Some scholars have maintained that what we have in the Koran is not a systematic code of law but rather moral principles or maxims (e.g., 4:1-5). I believe that they were meant to be or at least to have the force of positive law (e.g., 4:12). The legalism of the Koran is consciously and explicitly a development of certain aspects of Mosaic law: a reform of Mosaic law, if you wish to adopt the Koranic viewpoint. But while God Himself does not change, His laws for humanity do. Thus, we find certain commandments cancelled or abrogated by later commandments in the Koran (e.g., 2:106). In the Muslim view, these commandments must change because the eternal has to legislate for the non-eternal. If the conditions of man change, then the laws of men must change, a development in Islam carried to its extreme by the mystics.

And this, of course, marks a convenient point of transition to my fourth and final theme. This is the aspect of the Koran which I called at the beginning of my remarks its divine magic, its mysterious or miraculous aspect, the Sufi or mystic understanding or interpretation of the Koran. These mystics have been some of the most profound students of the Koran, the ones whose constant communion with God and the Koran have provided Islam with some of its most inspiring figures; these figures include Rābiʿah, al-Ḥallāj,* Ḥasan of Baṣra,* and Ibn al-ʿArabī.*

To begin with, the manner in which revelation descended upon Muḥammad is clearly reminiscent of a mystic trance. In these trances, the Prophet seemed to be uttering revelation despite himself, was tormented when revelation was slow to come, and recovered from each trance completely exhausted. Muḥammad was overpowered by revelation in much the same way that a mystic is overpowered by the presence of God. Islamic mysticism, therefore, attempted to re-create something of the same spiritual experience that came to Muḥammad whenever revelation descended upon him: to relive the experiences of Muḥammad. The revelations of Muḥammad were normally auditory, but on two occasions, especially in the very early period of revelation, he had visions as well, the most powerful of which being the vision of the angel Gabriel immense on the horizon: "This is naught but a revelation revealed, taught him by one terrible in power and very strong; he stood poised, being on the higher horizon, then drew near and suspended hung, two bows'-length away, or nearer, then revealed to his servant that which he revealed" (53:4-10). The presence of the angel seemed to him to fill the skies: an inescapable apparition and a symbol of the even more immense presence of God. This vision was very precious to the mystics, later on, who were intent upon contemplating God by recreating Muḥammad's revelatory experiences in their own mystical journeys.

God through the self: this might be considered the Sufi motto. But also the self through God. This is the other side of the coin, so to speak, of Sufi contemplation. And here the chapter called Light (Chapter 24) was another very dear image to the Sufis. God is compared to a lamp in a niche whose light is eternal, self-sufficient, shining *within* each one of us. To find the light, man looks *inward* and finds that God is something happening within us. Here one needs to remember the poetic imagery of pre-Islamic Arabia. A common theme of that poetry is the journey of the lonely traveller across the desert by night, guided on his way by the stars or by the light of the lamps of solitary Christian hermits. The night journey of Muḥammad himself (Chapter 17) becomes a prototype of the mystic journey to God. Thus, powerful literary images of ancient pre-Islamic Arabian poetry are transformed by the Koran into visions of God. But Muḥammad is not a man possessed, nor is he a poet, according to the Koran. And many scholars of religion have noted how often prophets have been confused with poets by their contemporaries and how often prophets have indignantly refused to be so identified.

However, the Koran possesses at least one characteristic in common with poetry, namely the difficulty of translation. The reason why the Koran itself is so difficult to translate is because its language presupposes what the poet T. S. Eliot calls an "auditory imagination," where the ring of its words, rhymes, and phrases penetrates below the conscious levels of thought and meaning; to quote Eliot: "sinking to the most primitive and forgotten, returning to the origin and bringing something back, seeking the beginning and the end." These words of Eliot may, I think, be happily applied to the language of the Koran, its magic, its miraculous nature.

The Koran is not an easy book to read or understand. It seems at every point to be making severe demands on both man's intellect as well as his imagination. A superstitious Muslim can pick it up, open a page at random, and then read the first verse that catches his eye to see how a particular endeavor will turn out. A mystic, however, can pick it up and, through the contemplation of its universe, use it as a guide to God.

Chapter Three

MUḤAMMAD AND HIS COMMUNITY

Ḥadīth

If we define the Koran as the record of the relationship between God and mankind, we may define *Ḥadīth* as the record of the relationship between the prophet and his people, Muḥammad and his *umma*, or community of followers. In fact, much of the inner vitality of Islam as a religion is derived from this dynamic relationship. I use the word dynamic here in an attempt to suggest a contrast between these two records. For, while there is a meta-historical divine finality about the Koran, both as a text and as a message, the *Ḥadīth* does not possess this same divine finality. The *Ḥadīth* is the record of the first two centuries of a historic relationship, and like all historic relationships, it passed through various stages until it was finally set down by Muslim scholars in the ninth century in the form we possess today.

Another point of contrast between the Koran and *Ḥadīth* is that whereas the Koran is non-contemporaneous in tone, emphasizing the eternity of the individual response to the Divine reality, and with God at all times at the very center of the stage, *Ḥadīth* is a far more personal and contemporaneous document of the early Muslim community. The Koran talks of man in the abstract: the *Ḥadīth* is full of real persons struggling with concrete problems. In the Koran, the emphasis is on individual responsibility. In *Ḥadīth*, the emphasis is on the religious needs of the community. The Koran has a predominantly theological spirit: the spirit of *Ḥadīth* is social and legal. The Koran is the book of God, "the book" for short. The *Ḥadīth* is the "book" of Muḥammad. Some of these contrasts will be developed later but I shall merely remind you at this stage that the *Ḥadīth* stands next to the Koran in importance as a source of the Islamic "law of life," or *sharīʿa*.

Ḥadīth in Arabic means report, written or oral. But just as the Koran is *the* book for Muslims, so *the Ḥadīth* refers to the reports of the sayings and doings of the Prophet Muḥammad. In the form in which we have it today, the *Ḥadīth* was edited by a number of renowned traditionists in the ninth century. Six works or collections of *Ḥadīth* became generally accepted as standard and were recognized by the Muslim community as authentic. Of these six, two in particular acquired especial esteem, the collections of Bukhārī* (d. 870) and Muslim* (d. 875). Hence, these two are often referred to as the two *Ṣaḥīḥs,* i.e., the two most accurate among the *Ḥadīth* collections.

To begin with, it is important to remember that the *Ḥadīth* collections preserve for us not only a record of what Muḥammad actually said or did but also a record of what his community in its first two centuries of existence *believed* that he said and did. In other words, the *Ḥadīth* contains a record of the historical Muḥammad as well as Muḥammad the image. The *Ḥadīth* preserves the past but also reads the present into the past—the present in this case being the concerns and experiences of the Muslim community as these had evolved by the ninth century. So the *Ḥadīth* can be used as a guide to understanding the historical Muḥammad as well as a guide to understanding the evolution of Muslim piety from the seventh to the ninth centuries. Both these aspects of *Ḥadīth* must be understood and kept in mind if we wish to have a total and accurate view of it.

This distinction between Muḥammad the man and Muḥammad the image is not a modern one. It was perfectly obvious to these same renowned traditionists who edited the *Ḥadīth* collections. The problem for them was not what to include in these collections but rather what to exclude. By the ninth century, the *Ḥadīths* circulating throughout the Islamic world and purporting to go back to the Prophet himself numbered in the millions. The task for these editors was to sift this vast mass of reports and to choose from among them those *Ḥadīths* they felt most probably emanated from the Prophet himself. The methodology they employed will be discussed later. These men, however, practiced rigorous criticism in their choice and were themselves satisfied that the *Ḥadīths* chosen were probably the most authentic from the historical point of view. Nevertheless, even with the most rigorous of them, the problem was not primarily one of historical accuracy. For they were also interested in preserving for their community a record of exemplary or normative Muslim behavior. They were aware of the fact that some of the *Ḥadīths* included were spurious, but they included them nonetheless because of their value as moral guides or maxims for the benefit of the community. Accordingly, we must not think of these *Ḥadīth* compilers as historians in the modern or even pre-modern sense nor did they conceive of their activity as exclusively or even primarily historical. You will see this when you read even a little *Ḥadīth*, for most *Ḥadīth* collections are divided into chapters and sections, each of which deals with one aspect of Muslim religious life. The sayings and doings of the Prophet are grouped *under* these chapter headings (e.g., Faith, Ritual Purity, Prayer, the Alms-tax, Fasting, and so forth). The primary interest of these *Ḥadīth* compilers is the good Muslim life; and what Muḥammad had to say about each aspect is fitted into the overall pattern, which in its totality constitutes a manual of that good life. Therefore, the question as to how much of the *Ḥadīth* is genuine and how much is not is really a specialized topic, of primary concern to students of Muḥammad's life and achievements, and I shall touch upon it only in passing in the course of these remarks. To separate Muḥammad the man from Muḥammad the image may be essential for a historical account of Muḥammad's life, but it is not essential for an appreciation of the scope and method of *Ḥadīth*.

I propose to deal with three themes in relation to *Ḥadīth*. The first is the historical experiences of the Muslim *umma*, especially as these are reflected in the *Ḥadīth*. By necessity, I shall be brief in this regard. My aim is not so much to narrate the history of the first 200 years of Islam but rather to point to a few of the major problems encountered by the community, which constitute the historical background of the society in which *Ḥadīth* developed. The second theme is the development of the *Ḥadīth* itself as a branch of Muslim religious learning and the evolution of *Ḥadīth* methodology. My third theme will be what one might call the spirit of the *Ḥadīth*, the world view that is encountered in it. Of course, all three topics are intimately related one to the other, and there may be some unavoidable overlap which I hope to minimize. Additionally, some of these remarks will be relevant not just to the understanding of *Ḥadīth* but also to the development of Islamic culture as a whole in the classical period.

To begin with, the historical background. It is important to keep in mind when we review the historical development of the Muslim community in its first two centuries of existence that many of these developments were accidental and unforeseen. Later Muslim writers or scholars often looked back upon these developments and interpreted them in a manner that would suggest that these developments followed a certain predetermined pattern, as if to argue that the hand of God was evident in setting the Muslim community along the path that it was later to follow. Nor is this type of historical argumentation peculiar to Muslim scholars, for it is quite common among, say, some Catholic historians who argue that the Papacy similarly followed a predetermined path.

Historical objectivity, however, as well as the evidence available, point to an evolutionary course of events that could at any point have followed a different path. The historian's task, says E. H. Carr, is to ask why things happened the way they did and why what could have happened did not in fact happen. In connection with the history of the early Muslim community, almost the very first problem that the community had to face was the problem of its continued existence. Should it continue to exist and if so in what form? Should it possess a political leadership and if so of what type? Answers eventually were found to both these questions, but these answers were not readily at hand. To give one example, when Abū Bakr* received the homage of the Muslim community as the first Caliph, or "deputy" to Muḥammad, voices were heard to say that this election was in fact an accident, a "fluke" *(falta)*. This is what a witty contemporary poet had to say on the subject:

> We obeyed the Prophet while he was amongst us
> But, servants of God, what has Abū Bakr to do with us?
> Will he, when he dies, bequeath the Caliphate to Bakr?
> This, I swear to God, will truly break our back.

It was a poet's way of making fun of the whole episode, but it illustrates the accidental manner in which this truly momentous event was viewed by contemporaries. Interestingly enough, the accidental nature of it is also found in *Ḥadīth*.

As regards early Islamic history, then, we must not only see it within its own historical framework. We must also remember that these early historical experiences of the *umma* were almost as important in their significance for Islamic history and culture as the life of Muḥammad himself. If we pursue our discussion of the problem of political power, for example, we find that the historical experiences preceded the political theory. The theorists in this case were scholars of later generations who looked back upon the political history of their community and deduced therefrom what one might call the political norm or the political theory. This suggests that at the time of the Prophet's death, the Muslim *umma* had little to go on by way of guidance in such vital questions as the legitimacy of political power. It was left up to the various factions within the *umma* to appeal to various and often contradictory principles in their attempt to justify their pursuit of power. Certain groups, for example, gave their loyalty to the house of ʿAlī, perhaps reflecting the ancient Arabian custom of allegiance to a specific clan of leadership. Others believed that the ideal period was the thirty or so years of the first four "rightly guided" Caliphs (632-661). Others paid allegiance to the House of the Umayyads,* the ancient merchant aristocracy of Mecca re-emerging in an Islamic garb. Still others rejected all leadership except the leadership of the most "pious," however that may be defined. From these various and conflicting allegiances, there grew the earliest political parties in Islam. Eventually, many were to develop into religious sects; here, again, the politics preceding the theology. Echoes of all these views are found in *Ḥadīth*.

Another subject echoed in *Ḥadīth* is that of social and economic life and its norms. Here, too, the Muslim community was left without much guidance. Thus, the economic and taxation systems of Muḥammad's days may have been appropriate for the Muslim *umma* during its Arabian infancy. When this same *umma* had conquered a vast empire, the problems facing it as well as its own historical evolution had acquired new and often perplexing dimensions. Ancient centers of civilization were conquered to which the conquering Arab Muslims had to adapt themselves with little specific guidance from their revealed text. The new wealth and the new social horizons meant the need for new answers to problems of life in what became an essentially urban and commercial environment. This, too, is echoed in *Ḥadīth*.

A third subject is that of religious institutions. How was the faith to be carried on from one generation of Muslims to the next? Who was empowered to determine whether a specific way of life or action was in conformity with Islam or not? These, too, were historical problems, and the answer to them was often found in the actual historical experiences of a class of men known as the *ʿulamāʾ*, or religious scholars. Their exclusion from politics gave them over the years an exaggerated sense of their own importance to the continued welfare of Islam, but their increasing association with the administration of justice in the ninth century gave them an "esprit de corps," a sense of belonging to a class that felt itself responsible for the maintenance of the Muslim way of life. It was this class, of course, that produced the *Ḥadīth*, and their own urban roots and commercial interests are reflected in its pages.

These, then, are some of the major historical problems encountered by the community in its first two centuries of existence. It is necessary for us to keep these problems in mind because of their relevance to the genesis and development of *Ḥadīth*, to which I shall now turn.

As regards the actual composition of *Ḥadīth*, the issue may be clarified if we examine the literary environment in which it grew. Thus, it has been pointed out by many scholars that sacred prose literature was not unknown among the Arabians of Muḥammad's time. The Koran alludes to the existence of such a body of literature when Muḥammad himself is accused by his enemies of repeating the "fairy-tales of the ancients." The name given to much of this literature in Arabic was *isrā'īliyyāt* (stories of the Israelites), an undifferentiated mass of stories circulating among both Jews and Christians mainly from South Arabia, in the form of commentaries perhaps, or amplifications of Biblical materials: a mass of both written and oral religious folklore. There was, therefore, nothing surprising in the early Muslim community's resort to a similar literary activity, namely, the recording of the Prophet's sayings and doings by members of the Muslim community even in his own lifetime. This recording activity, it has now been established, was both written and oral, and it encompassed not just the Prophet's life but also the lives and doings of his earliest companions. So the earliest *Ḥadīth* was in one respect undifferentiated, in the sense that it took in Muḥammad's life as well as the lives of his pious followers. Opposition to this recording activity was soon bypassed.

Nevertheless, modern scholarship has shown that even in the earliest days, special importance was attached by these compilers to *Ḥadīth* from the Prophet. Two reasons may be suggested for this, the one logically and historically connected with the other. The first is that the prestige of Muḥammad himself tended to grow with the passage of years. The dramatic nature of the conquests served only to enhance his standing and the truth of his mission in the eyes of his *umma*. His whole life was endowed with an aura of almost superhuman achievement, a development that he himself kept carefully in check while he lived. The minutest details of his everyday life were recorded and studied. His life was quickly to become the exemplary Muslim life, and the true believer could do no better than to imitate that life even in its most inconsequential details. With early *Ḥadīth*, therefore, it was a simple case of supply and demand. The believers demanded guidance, and Muḥammad's life supplied it.

The second reason for the growth of *Ḥadīth* was the collective demand, especially by the ruling circles of the new empire, for guidance in larger matters of state. How provinces were to be governed, how taxes were to be collected, what rules and regulations should govern intra- and extra-Muslim relations were all matters of daily practical policy for which any guidance whatever was welcome. The motive here was not so much the need for individual religious guidance but rather the requirements of practical policy of the state itself. Here, too, the tendency, with time, was to pay special heed to the example of the Prophet, even though the examples set by the first four caliphs were also sought after, because it was felt that these four most faithfully practiced his own example.

Ḥadīth, therefore, was to grow by leaps and bounds in the first two centuries of Islam and to echo the expansion of the horizons of Islam in the political as well as the religious realms. The systematization and rationalization of this body of religious literature itself underwent a historical evolution, culminating in the ninth century, when the subject matter as well as the methodology of *Ḥadīth* were finally fixed. As regards subject matter, the *Ḥadīth* encompassed practically the whole spectrum of Islamic life, and I shall say a little about its spirit later. As regards its methodology, perhaps the earliest form of *Ḥadīth* was the family collection, i.e., the type of *Ḥadīth* that descended from parent to child or from teacher to student, although opinions on this differ among modern scholars. Whatever the case may be, a distinctive methodology of transmission was evolved, which I shall discuss briefly, but which was of tremendous influence on the methodology of many other Islamic sciences that may be considered offshoots of the science of *Ḥadīth*, such as jurisprudence, historiography, and biography.

This methodology as it had evolved by the ninth century was based on the assumption that the truth of a particular *Ḥadīth* depended largely, though not exclusively, on its line of transmission. This concept may very well have been rooted in the pre-Islamic custom of poetic transmission, where poets would entrust their poetry to certain transmitters who were best qualified to transmit the poetry of the master to a third party, and so on. Every *Ḥadīth* was thus divided into two parts: the actual substance of the report itself *(matn)* and the line of transmitters *(isnād)*. The ninth-century *Ḥadīth* compilers took both into account in determining the veracity of a given *Ḥadīth*, and elaborate rules and regulations were developed to test this, which need not concern us here. Accordingly, this methodology was based on the view, also elaborated in the ninth century, that the surest way in which one could ascertain the accuracy of a given report about the past was to ascertain the manner in which that report was handed down from one generation to the next. This view was at the heart of *Ḥadīth* methodology and can also be seen in the historical literature written under the influence of *Ḥadīth*. It did not exclude testing the substance of any given *Ḥadīth*, e.g., whether the *Ḥadīth* in question conformed with what was revealed in the Koran. But it did attach greater importance to the manner of transmission, and *Ḥadīth* therefore generated, among other things, an interest in biographical lists or dictionaries, first about the transmitters themselves and later of the worthy men of the whole *umma*, a genre of historical writing that was to flourish right down to the nineteenth century and beyond.

Let me now turn to my third theme, which is what I earlier on called the "spirit" of *Ḥadīth*. Two points may be emphasized before we proceed: first, the socioeconomic background of the *Ḥadīth* compilers and, second, the fact that the great majority of the *Ḥadīth* material relates to Muḥammad's life in Medina rather than to his earlier life in Mecca. As regards the first point, one must remember that much of the *Ḥadīth* was compiled in its final shape by scholars working in the new Muslim cities of Iraq and the east, places like Baghdad, Baṣra, and Kūfa. The spirit of these men was urban, commercial, rationalist, and pragmatic. The new dynasty under which they worked, the Baghdad Abbasids* (750-1258), was intent upon forging a new unity among the Muslim *umma*, a new religious policy or equilibrium, one might say, which claimed to have reestablished equality for all Muslims. The early caliphs of this dynasty cultivated the scholarly class, and through the establishment of the judiciary corps, gave this class a more secure place in the religious life of the empire. Slowly but surely, these scholars adopted a conciliatory stance among themselves and attempted to create a new religious synthesis, just as their Abbasid masters were attempting to create a new political one. I do not mean to suggest that *Ḥadīth* compilation was a reflection of Abbasid political propaganda. It was, however, a reflection of the conciliatory atmosphere of their times and of their own urban, commercial, and pragmatic concerns.

This, of course, is related to my second point, namely that the *Ḥadīth* we possess relates in its great majority to Muḥammad's Medinese period. *Ḥadīth*, therefore, has tended to leave its imprint on Islam by concentrating on a period of the Prophet's life when he was legislating for his community, with an emphasis on man's deeds. The good deed is at the heart of Islamic life in *Ḥadīth*. "The good deed is multiplied 7000 times—the bad deed is recorded only once," says one *Ḥadīth*. Even an atom of virtue is enough to release man from hell. Faith is a matter ultimately between man and his Creator. Trying to find their way through a maze of theological and political conflict, the *Ḥadīth* editors were motivated by their desire to preserve the unity of the *umma* at all costs. The Prophet, therefore, is depicted as lenient with his community as regards the requirements of faith (e.g., the story of Moses, whom he met on his night journey, advising him to ask God to reduce the number of daily prayers required and the many other *Ḥadīths* of the Prophet speeding up, for example, the time of prayer in order to lighten the burden of the sick or needy). I am not passing any judgment here on the historical accuracy of such *Ḥadīths* nor need we be concerned with this problem if we are discussing its spirit. But Islam in *Ḥadīth* is depicted as a religion that imposes a minimum of burdens on the believer.

At the same time, however, the unity of the *umma* is stressed repeatedly. Thus, for example, it is important for the believers to pray *in ranks* (cf., the angels ranged *in ranks* in the Koran [89:22]). This unity of the believers is to be maintained as against the disputations of either Muslim heretics or other religious communities. Muḥammad himself attaches enormous importance to the unity of his *umma*, which is most clearly manifested in congregational prayer, and the Day of Judgment is a day when the Prophet will appear to lead his *umma* drawn up in ranks, and other prophets will follow suit with their *ummas*. This, I presume, explains the hostility found in both the Koran and the *Ḥadīth* towards the Bedouin way of life, suspect essentially because of its chaotic nomadism, to which is contrasted the regimented urbanism of the true believers. As for such controversial figures in early Arab Islamic history as ʿAlī or ʿUthmān,* the *Ḥadīth* tends to exonerate them from all blame and at the same time to check the extravagant claims of their supporters. Here, again, the tendency towards reconciliation is obvious.

The portrait of Muḥammad himself in the *Ḥadīth* is very human and attractive. True, the aura that surrounded his person after his death is reflected in some *Ḥadīths*, which depict him as a miracle worker. In some of these miracles, we find clear echoes of the New Testament miracles of Jesus, e.g., the miracle of the loaves. But the overall impression that one gains of his personality is a human one. The minutest details of his personal life and habits are described—including what to do if a fly lands in the soup! But it is also quite simple to draw up a psychological portrait of Muḥammad and of his personal likes and dislikes. Here is a rapid list of these. He liked perfume, personal cleanliness, certain foods, precious stones, laughter, horses, children. He disliked bad smells, dogs and pigs, pictures, drunkenness, physical ugliness, gold, proud people. From *Ḥadīth*, we know almost exactly what he looked like, his manner of speech, how he walked and dressed, and so forth. Much of this is undoubtedly genuine historical material, and it tended to stamp the taste and fashions of the early Muslim community, indeed to influence the tastes of the Muslim *umma* both past and present.

But the *Ḥadīth* also reflects a sense of the moral deterioration of the *umma* from Muḥammad's generation onward. The golden age, so to speak, is behind us, at least from a moral point of view. The believer, therefore, can do no better than to imitate the moral example of Muḥammad and his generation. He must avoid civil discord, and *Ḥadīth* tends to preach political quietism. Meanwhile, it is up to the *ʿulamāʾ* to preserve religious scholarship from one age to the next. Thus, one of the pointers to the coming of the end will be the disappearance of religious knowledge, the invasion of the cities by nomads, and the upsetting of the natural order of the family. Family life, communal order, and religious scholarship—these are the three foundations of Islamic life as established in *Ḥadīth*.

Fiqh, or Jurisprudence

It has already been argued that in any discussion of Islamic culture, the greatest importance must be attached to *Fiqh*, or jurisprudence, for two reasons—the first quantitative and the second qualitative. Quantitatively speaking, more works on *Fiqh* were produced by this civilization than on any other single Islamic science. Qualitatively, *Fiqh* has been and remains the most basic part of the Islamic curriculum. Therefore, a few words of explanation are in order as to the relatively short space that I have assigned to *Fiqh* in these pages.

To begin with, I shall not be concerned with religious law as such but rather with its conceptual foundations, with what in Arabic is called *Uṣūl al-fiqh*, the foundations of jurisprudence, a science that merges into theology. Secondly, I shall be primarily concerned with only one man, al-Shāfiʿī, a ninth-century scholar who is a major figure in the evolution of this science and whose works have come down to us together with the school of law that he founded and which still flourishes today.

The word *Fiqh* is generally translated as jurisprudence, a particularly happy translation because the word *Fiqh* includes the primary sense of prudence in, or knowledge of, the Islamic "law of life" or *Sharīʿa*. Here, too, the ninth century was a critical one in witnessing the systematization and elaboration of *Fiqh*, as of so many other branches of Islamic culture. This century is the one I have called elsewhere the "Age of the Great Debate." It was an age when Muslim scholars took stock of what had passed before, and this stock-taking was perhaps nowhere as extensive and elaborate as in the field of *Fiqh*. The Muslims of that century were intent, not only upon defining the conceptual foundations of their culture but also upon defending it from both internal schism and external attack.

The three major conceptual problems facing Muslim jurists of that century were the following: First, *What* is the Law? Second, *Who* elaborates the Law? Third, *How* is the Law to be elaborated? All three questions had, of course, received answers in the course of Islamic history up to the ninth century. Therefore, the great achievement of the ninth-century lawyers was not one of originality so much as of system-building and rationalization. Ancient schools of law had indeed existed since the late seventh century, attaching themselves either to geographical locations such as the Ḥijāz and Iraq, or to masters whose authority was followed with varying degrees of strictness. These ancient schools may perhaps best be understood as loose movements or even states of mind, conditioned by the historical experiences or the locality of the men that produced them rather than the strict ways of law *(madhhab)* that they later on became. Accordingly, one might speak of the ninth century as the critical transitional stage between the earlier and more diffuse ancient schools and the later and more systematic *madhhabs* or stricter legal ways.

To turn now to the first question, namely: *What* is the *Sharīʿa*, or Law of Islamic Life as I have been translating it? The primary answer to this question was as final for the ancients (i.e., pre-ninth-century scholars) as it was for Shāfiʿī, viz., the Koran. The Koran is regarded as the supreme guide to the law of Islamic life—and I use the word "guide" on purpose to suggest the legal attitude adopted towards the Koran, not so much as a legal code, but rather as a guide whereby the Muslim, in the words of Shāfiᶜī, can grow in his understanding of the text and in deducing from that text the guidelines of his religious life. As many scholars have pointed out, this attitude tends to blur the distinction between "religion" and "law" and to subsume both under *Sharīᶜa*, which is why I have translated this as "law of life." The very finality of the Koranic text guaranteed the acceptance of that text as the fountainhead of the *Sharīᶜa*.

But to gain in understanding of this *Sharīᶜa* is also to accept the Koranic view that wisdom *(ḥikma)* is an essential part of faith. It is the wisdom that enables the Muslim to recognize, rationalize, and systematize the "law of life," in other words, to use the Koran as a guide in further elaboration of the *Sharīᶜa*. Here, too, it was recognized from the earliest times that this wisdom was most perfectly manifested in Muḥammad, the Prophet, who was not merely a messenger of God but the wise exponent of God's revelation. To believe in God is also to believe in the exponential wisdom of His Prophet. Shāfiᶜī's emphasis on this point was not new, for we have seen earlier that there were always Muslims who attached special importance to the Prophet's *Ḥadīth* even while they collected the *Ḥadīth* of his pious followers as well.

The *Ḥadīth* for Shāfiᶜī, therefore, constitutes an exemplary elaboration of the Koran and must therefore be accepted as the second source of *Sharīᶜa*. This is because, in strictly rational terms, there can be no contradiction between the Divine Revelation on the one hand and its own exemplary interpretation at the hands of the Prophet on the other. The distinction is between principle and practice, general guideline and specific injunction. Thus, Shāfiᶜī, for example, in discussing the laws of inheritance in the Koran shows how the practice of the Prophet specifies that the inheritor must not be a murderer or a slave. Similarly, for the crime of theft, the Koran prescribes the general punishment of hand-cutting. But the practice of Muḥammad excludes from this punishment the theft of dates and of what is worth less than ¼ dinar in value. The general principle here is that the contradictions found in the Prophet's *Ḥadīths* as well as in certain Koranic verses, are only apparent, not real. Such contradictions are, therefore, at all times a reflection of the frailty of human understanding or faultiness of transmission rather than being a reflection of any inherent shortcomings of the Koran or the *Ḥadīth*, both of which are, for Shāfiᶜī, monolithic and complementary systems. If there are contradictons, then deeper understanding and further investigation would reveal that both the Koran and *Ḥadīth* provide for self-correction, i.e., they both contain the means by which internal reconciliation of one specific ruling with another can be achieved.

But Shāfiᶜī was well aware of the differences that had torn the Muslim community over the interpretation of certain aspects of *Sharīᶜa*. His insistence on the primacy of *Ḥadīth* from the Prophet and his pious community may conceivably owe something to Shīᶜite jurists who, from the beginning, had followed ᶜAlī's example of abiding only by the practice of the Prophet rather than by the practice of the Prophet and his first two successors. Additionally, the spirit of Shāfiᶜī's work was the spirit of the specialized scholar who recognized that legal scholarship must be confined to the few learned men of the community rather than to any Muslim whose fancy drove him to interpret the *Sharīᶜa*. Therefore, in answer to the second question posed earlier, viz., "Who elaborates the Law?", Shāfiᶜī insisted that only the elite among Muslim scholars could do so. This insistence on the central role of specialized scholars is, of course, in conformity with the increasing institutionalization of Muslim scholarship that was becoming apparent in his own day and age, which was the middle Abbasid period.

There remain, however, gray areas in *Sharīᶜa*, where clear guidance both in the Koran and *Ḥadīth* are lacking, and this leads to the third question, viz., "How is the Law to be elaborated?" Shāfiᶜī was prone to minimize the seriousness of these gray areas, which had given rise to differences in the practice of the *umma*. These gray areas, he says, can either be left to stand, e.g., where they concern minor points of ritual, or else interpretation is to be exercised in elucidating them. Here, interpretation had, by Shāfiᶜī's day, been defined as resting upon two foundations: *qiyās* (or analogical reasoning) and *ijmāᶜ* (or consensus). Both were accepted by Shāfiᶜī as valid means of interpreting the Law, but both were restricted by him in certain important respects. The first restriction, of course, has to do with Shāfiᶜī's own limited and elitist view of his profession, i.e., that this is an activity to be engaged in only by the few, not by the many. The second restriction was to argue, as he did, that analogical reasoning can either be simple, e.g., of the type that logicians might call the major and minor premise, or complex, e.g., where the major premise is not one but several. Here Shāfiᶜī postulated certain principles to be followed, e.g., that preference was to be shown for earlier and more trustworthy reports over later ones, or for reports that are closer in spirit to the Koran and *Ḥadīth* than others. Shāfiᶜī also argued for a literalist and general interpretation of the Koran and *Ḥadīth* where there is no reason to suppose such injunctions to be particular to time and place. In other words, particularity is to be inferred only if warranted by the context. To allow full latitude of interpretation on the grounds that such latitude is beneficial to the community *(istiḥsān)* was a principle that Shāfiᶜī rejected decisively, because he saw in this an area of interpretation in which anyone could engage, therefore leading to legislative chaos. Here again, only specialist scholars, if anyone, could pronounce judgment, and this, only in accordance with strict principles of analogical reasoning derived from the Koran and *Ḥadīth*.

The last source of interpretation was the principle of *ijmāᶜ*, consensus, which too had evolved prior to Shāfiᶜī's days. The principle of consensus had been resorted to by earlier schools of law to justify the validity of their own interpretations as against the interpretations of other schools. For Shāfiᶜī it was really a question of all or nothing. The consensus either had to be a consensus of the entire Muslim community on any one particular point of law, or it was nothing more than sophistication expounded by members of one particular school. In other words, Shāfiᶜī saw this as little more than self-perpetuating provincialism, no more binding than social custom:

> He who holds the opinions of the community of Muslims is a member of their community. . . . It is in a sect that error arises. In the community at large, however, no error can arise as regards the true significance of the Koran, prophetic *Ḥadīth*, or analogy.

The great achievement of Shāfiᶜī, therefore, rests on his attempt to cut through the mass of established custom by insisting on the primacy of the Koran and *Ḥadīth* as the two supreme guides to the Islamic law of life. All else was to him secondary and derivative. Only these two were primary. The accumulated popular and administrative practice of the Islamic community was not to be regarded as normative. Where such practices diverged from the Koran and *Ḥadīth*, they had to be rejected, regardless of the respectability they had gained among their followers. Human reason had a role to play in legal elaboration, but this role was restricted by the manifest clarity of the two supreme guiding texts of the community.

Among the many historical consequences of Shāfiᶜī's work was the fact that later *Fiqh*, in its majority, came to concentrate on prophetic *Ḥadīth* even more than on the Koran. It was perhaps also due to him that the two areas of Islamic *Fiqh*, the area of unchanging norms and regulations of Koran and *Ḥadīth* and the area of putative norms and regulations of communal or individual opinion, were more strictly determined than ever before.

Chapter Four

ISLAMIC PAIDEIA

Adab

A phenomenon as remarkable as the speed of the Islamic conquests was the speed with which the Arabic language supplanted the original languages of the conquered territories. This linguistic conquest was certainly far more thorough than the spread of Islam as a religion. We know that even as late as the ninth century, Islam was still the religion of a minority, for example in Egypt. On the other hand, Arabic very quickly became the language of the majority of the inhabitants of the Arab Muslim empire, in what appears to have been a unique case in the history of language, outstripping the flag. This is all the more surprising when we remember that the languages that Arabic supplanted were themselves of immense cultural richness (Greek and Syriac, Pahlavi and Coptic) and that apart from the Koran and some poetry, Arabic had neither the richness nor the volume possessed by its competitors. Various explanations have been offered by modern scholars for this unusual linguistic conquest, but none is fully satisfying, probably because of the historically unique nature of that phenomenon and the lack of any historically useful parallels. Perhaps the very speed and the finality of the conquest was such as to shatter the "sound barrier" of the original languages! Or perhaps the Koranic self-confidence of the conquerors as well as their early imperviousness to other cultures forced the conquered to deal with them on their own terms, both political as well as linguistic. Or perhaps the Ḥijāzī Arabic of the Koran, fresh from its pre-Islamic triumphs over the whole of Arabia as well as the Iraqi and Syrian countrysides, still possessed the élan of the newly victorious. Or perhaps all cultures in their youth tend to be somewhat deaf. Whatever the explanation may be for this phenomenon, we can study its effects with relative ease. One such effect of this linguistic conquest was to create, for a century or more, a hiatus in the cultural traditions of the conquered peoples. These traditions did not vanish, of course, but were suppressed, in the Freudian sense, to reappear later in an Arabic/Islamic form. Another effect was that non-Arab Muslims (and even non-Arab non-Muslims) quickly assimilated themselves into Arabic culture and, within a short span of time, were able to enrich it with their own contributions and help to transform it into a cosmopolitan civilization.

What literature did the Muslim Arabs bring with them out of the peninsula? First and foremost, the Koran, but also a relatively large body of pre-Islamic poetry, in addition to a tradition of urban literacy. The interaction among these three elements and the exposure of the Arab conquerors to the ancient cultures of the conquered lands were to constitute the groundwork for later Arabic literature. It is possible, therefore, to speak of two literary traditions, the one sacred and the other secular, existing side by side from the beginning. This distinction between sacred and secular at times gets blurred, especially in the early periods, but the fact that the line between them was rather vague does not mean that the distinction between the two did not exist.

Let me develop some of these themes and try, whenever possible, to situate them within their historical context. To begin with, the tension between the sacred and the secular is best evident in the Koran's attitude to poetry and poets (e.g., in the concluding verses of Chapter 26). These suspicions were prompted by Muḥammad's own insistence that his revelations had nothing to do with the versification of Arabian soothsayers. They were also prompted by Muḥammad's personal feelings of antipathy to this bragging and boastful group, lionized and feared by tribesmen and city people alike. As a group, these poets were supremely arrogant: they could literally make or break men's reputations. Their role in Arabia was not solely confined to aesthetics. Their verses were remembered from one generation to the next and often wielded tremendous influence upon "public opinion" in the peninsula. It was perhaps this sociopolitical role that irked Muḥammad most about them. Their proud and individualistic spirit had to be checked by the more submissive and communal spirit that Islam inculcated. The pathos as well as the tragic heroism of their verses, their glorification of individual and tribal prowess, in short the epic mood of their poetry had to be redirected or rechannelled into the service of the new Islamic ideology. Many a pagan virtue became a Muslim vice and was flatly condemned as belonging to a barbarous and ignorant past.

However, in many ways it was too late. For when Islam appeared, Arabian poetry had already achieved a very high standard of development in both content and form. Despite Islam's early antipoetical mood, Arabian poetry was very well established in Arab consciousness. It had become a reflection of a whole way of life, often associated in the minds of later generations with an era and a locality that were the cradle of their own religion, indeed of their whole cultural heritage. A place was found for it alongside sacred literature, and with time this place became an honored one. Among other uses, this poetry came to be prized by the early religious scholars as a storehouse of linguistic examples, essential for a proper philological understanding of the Koranic text. This body of pre-Islamic poetry has always been cherished. At times it was revered almost as much as the Koran. At others, it was ridiculed as uncouth and unsophisticated. But the nostalgia it inspired for a simple, heroic, individualist, and (largely but not wholly) desert way of life has remained an essential part of Arabic poetic sensibility down to the present day. The Umayyad dynasty in the 89 years of its existence helped greatly to foster this sense of nostalgia. Many Umayyad rulers were themselves accomplished poets, and their style of life often resembled the tempestuous lives of the early epic poets they so much admired. Their frequent escape to their desert palaces was a reflection of their homesickness for a supposedly freer and happier mode of life. But this was not merely the nostalgia of a ruling class. The whole gamut of Umayyad society was still in a state of flux between the tribal and the sedentary mode of existence. Entire tribes would pass back and forth between a sedentary and a nomadic way of life. In fact, nomadism was never very far from the urban surface of life throughout the classical period and well into modern times. It is this tension between the two modes of life that explains the perennial popularity of ancient Arabian poetry. Accordingly, religious scholarship soon had to accommodate this secular poetry.

The scope of these pages does not, unfortunately, allow me to deal with later Arabic poetry in detail. Instead, I shall be concentrating on prose literature and confining myself largely within the limits of the eighth to tenth centuries. In the realm of prose, the religious stimulus was clearly far more in evidence—although here, too, a secular mood could also be detected, as I shall show later. Let me first recall a point while I was discussing the *Ḥadīth*, namely, the existence of a body of sacred prose literature written in Arabic during the lifetime of the Prophet. This non-Islamic prose tradition was continued in some sense by *Ḥadīth* and by a host of auxiliary sciences that developed parallel to, or out of, *Ḥadīth* itself. Thus, *Ḥadīth* inspired, but did not necessarily dominate, Arabic Islamic prose literature in its first century of existence and beyond. As we have seen, the Umayyads on the whole were keenly interested in their Arabian past and the *Ḥadīth* collected in their courts included not just *Ḥadīth* from the Prophet but a large mass of historical and mythical prose literature relating to both Arabian as well as non-Arabian antiquities. The literary interests of the Umayyads extended far beyond sacred literature to include a deep interest in history as a whole, motivated by aesthetic and antiquarian interests as well as pragmatic and political reasons of state.

In addition to Umayyad *Ḥadīth*, understood here to mean "antiquities" in general, another stimulus to the rise of a prose literature in Arabic was the vigorous movement of translation that began in earnest in the later years of the Umayyad dynasty and was closely associated with the ruling circles. Urban patterns of life had gained a firmer hold on the Arab Muslim conquerors, making them more susceptible to the cultural traditions of the regions over which they ruled. The two dominant cultural traditions were the Byzantine and the Persian. We know less about interactions with the first than we do about the second, partly because as early as the middle Umayyad period the whole center of gravity of the Arab Islamic Empire was shifting toward the East even while its capital remained in formerly Byzantine territory. But it was in the East, in what was formerly Persian Sasanid territory, that wealth and manpower was beginning to concentrate. And in literature proper, as opposed to, say, art, the Indian-Persian cultural traditions were beginning to exercise their effect, especially on the development of Arabic prose.

So side by side with the sacred prose literature, i.e., *Ḥadīth* and its auxiliary disciplines, there grew, largely through translation, a body of secular prose literature in late Umayyad times, and it is in this period, i.e., the middle of the eighth century, that the concept of *Adab* developed, loosely translated as Belles-Lettres. The tendency toward closer interaction with India-Persia was further strengthened when the Abbasids replaced the Umayyads and moved over to Baghdad, itself not far from the ancient Sasanid capital, thus actualizing a development that had already begun to take place in the later days of their predecessors.

We know little about the origins of *Adab* largely because the Abbasids systematically destroyed the cultural monuments of their predecessors—even though they were unable to destroy their poetry, which survived because of its strong association with oral transmission. So when we survey prose *Adab* historically, we have to pick up the thread from the early Abbasid period, where we find the genre already well developed at the hands of translators like Ibn al-Muqaffaʿ* and state secretaries like ʿAbd al-Ḥamīd al-Kātib.* These were men whose lives spanned the late Umayyad and early Abbasid periods. They were men close to the government, courtiers and state secretaries whose prose reflected the widening urban horizons of their society in general and of their political masters in particular. It was a period (mid-eighth century) when the epistle or prose essay was developed as a result either of direct translation from the Persian-Indian heritage or of the growing refinement of urban manners and complexities of bureaucracy. As a distinct social class, the royal secretaries were to emerge sooner than the class of *ʿulamāʾ*, or religious scholars, and thus took the lead in opening Arabic culture to foreign cultural influences.

This class of royal secretaries and courtiers was to continue to play a leading role in the development of *Adab*, providing adaptations and translations of Indian-Persian wisdom literature for the edification and amusement of their masters and of the sophisticated upper echelons of society, who imitated the fashions of the court and often had miniature courts of their own. The wisdom literature now available in Arabic included fables and proverbs, histories and myths—in short the "folk" as well as the "high" literature of earlier, especially Persian and Indian civilizations. What gave continuity to this activity was the fact that many of these state secretaries belonged to families of civil servants, many of whom found little difficulty, because of their expertise, in changing their allegiance from one dynasty to the next. By the ninth century, a mass of this wisdom literature had accumulated and, in the process, had greatly enriched the Arabic language, where the enormous flexibility of its verbal forms was found eminently suitable to express the finest shades of meaning. The stage was now set for the great *kultur kampf*, or cultural battle, that was to erupt in the ninth century.

From the viewpoint of the religious community, things had gone too far. Already in the late eighth century, the Abbasid court itself was shaken by a series of scandals involving some Abbasid princes who were found to be crypto-Manichaean *(zindīq)*. In other words, their enchantment with "foreign" literature had turned them into heretics. The opinions of religious scholars could not be ignored by the Abbasids and these heretics, together with the culture they espoused, were rooted out and executed. But this royal scandal was only the tip of the iceberg, for much more was involved than just a few princes and their cronies dabbling in foreign and anti-Islamic culture and literature. At stake was the whole cultural orientation of Arabic Islamic culture. Was this Islamic culture strictly to be confined to the religious sciences and Arabic philology that supported it, or was this culture to be broadened and opened up to include the "wisdom" of all nations? This was a complex cultural dilemma, fought out by the various protagonists at various levels. Cultural orientation was closely bound with religious orientation as well, and the *kultur kampf* that developed is perhaps best reflected in the *Adab* controversies of the ninth century.

To begin with, the claims advanced for this foreign literature were often extravagant. The cosmopolitan literature of non-Arab and non-Islamic culture became favorite reading of secretaries and courtiers, who sought foreign models. While they did not dare to attack Islam directly, they attacked the Arabic milieu from which Islam evolved, describing its manner of life as uncouth and caricaturing its nomadic values in particular as, at best, outdated and irrelevant. On the other side, the pious Muslim scholars saw in this a veiled attack upon Islam itself and upon its Arabian Prophet. They grew to be suspicious of all "foreign" cultures when compared with their own final revelation. What more wisdom is needed when one possessed the final and ultimate wisdom of God, expressed in "clear Arabic tongue"? And what further culture is needed than the ancient Arabian poetry, which helped to clarify and situate Islamic revelation? In the process of debating with each other, both sides were, of course, to enrich greatly the corpus of Arabic prose that had already become a flexible instrument of polemic.

Arabic culture versus Persian-Indian, sacred literature versus secular, urban life versus nomadism, and, to a lesser extent, one national sentiment versus another—all these were factors in the cultural war that was joined in the ninth century. Into the breach stepped Jāḥiẓ* (d. 869), and while we must not exaggerate his contribution to this cultural war—since it continued to rage long after his death—he, through the corpus of his writings, was to give a definition of *Adab* that exercised enormous influence on his literary successors and helped to clarify many of the basic cultural issues involved.

For Jāḥiẓ, *Adab* was 1) the total educational system of 2) a cultured Muslim who 3) took the whole world for his object of curiosity and knowledge. If we take this definition apart, we should arrive at a classical definition of *Adab* that was to remain normative for centuries. Let us first take the phrase "total educational system." Here *Adab* appears to be the equivalent of the Greek notion of *paideia*, where education becomes part of the moral character of man. It is total in the sense that only total knowledge can achieve this moral and educational transformation in the soul of the student. It is total also in the sense that *Adab* avoids what has been called "unilateral professionalism," or, to use a modern word, specialization. In other words, the *adīb*, or possessor of *Adab*, is at home in all branches of knowledge, without necessarily being a specialist in any one branch. Thus, while the notion of specialization is not excluded, it is subsumed under the notion of general knowledge. Accordingly, Jāḥiẓ was to argue that the style of *Adab* should be discursive. Instead of forcing the reader or listener to examine any one problem to the exclusion of all others, *Adab* leads the reader gently from one subject to another, intent upon holding his interest and not boring him with one-sided erudition or expertise. The style of *Adab* must also be a simple one. The vocabulary used must be down-to-earth and easily understood. Verbal gymnastics and neologisms must be avoided as artificial. *Adab* is a system for Jāḥiẓ, because knowledge itself occurs through repetition of experience or, to use a modern term, "reinforcement." A man learns, according to Jāḥiẓ, much like a horse or dog, i.e., through the repetition of experience until enough experience is accumulated to permit discrimination. It is experience that generates knowledge —reason only engenders discrimination of experience. Accordingly, *Adab* must include as much experience as possible, and the true *adīb* is the one who finally sifts through this mass of knowledge to arrive at wisdom.

The second part of the definition is the phrase "cultured Muslim." It is here that Jāḥiẓ made his direct contribution to the *kultur kampf* raging around him. For Jāḥiẓ, the acceptance of sacred literature (Koran, *Ḥadīth*, and their derivative sciences) as the foundation of Islamic culture was absolute. At the same time, he was impatient with the obscurantism of *Ḥadīth* scholars. He believed firmly that Islam was the heir of world culture in the same sense that the Islamic religion was the heir to all previous revelations. For the cultured Muslim, therefore, all past wisdom, whatever its source, was inherited by Islamic wisdom, which in fact had the job of preserving and developing that wisdom *ad infinitum*. His theory of cognition predisposed him to believe in the perpetual increase of knowledge. Therefore, the cultured Muslim should feel no religious compunction at all about absorbing all the wisdom of ancient nations because this was a part of his own heritage. It was, therefore, futile to engage in debate about the relative merit of Arab versus Persian or Indian culture. Each had made its own unique contribution to the civilization of Islam. Just as all past piety was by definition Muslim, so all past wisdom was by definition a precursor of Islamic wisdom. And while acknowledging a progressive improvement in knowledge, he was not particularly nostalgic about ancient Arabian poetry or antiquities, preferring to hold to the view that good literature as such was found in all eras, irrespective of whether that era was ancient or modern. In this resepct and through his theory of progress, Jāḥiẓ wanted to transcend the conservatism of the "ancients," who believed that the best wisdom was already behind them as well as the frivolity of the "moderns," who latched on to every novel fashion of the day and ridiculed the past as irrelevant and uncouth.

This brings us to the third element of the definition of *Adab*, namely Jāḥiẓ's wide-ranging interest and curiosity, which took the whole world of creation as its object. Here, Jāḥiẓ's *Book of Animals* is a good illustration of his limitless curiosity. This curiosity is at every turn reinforced by the Koranic injunction to investigate the "signs" of God, holding them up for examination and meanwhile examining the nature of knowledge itself and of its progress from the minutest to the most momentous, from the most trivial to the most weighty. Throughout this examination, Jāḥiẓ is well aware of the precarious nature of human cognition and how easy it is for the mind to fall prone to "disease" or "slumber," how important it is for man to be alert and curious, how intricate and complex God's creation can be—"a whole lifetime can be spent examining a mosquito's wing." The *adīb*, therefore, must put knowledge in front, not behind him. Islam for Jāḥiẓ was a cultural beginning not a cultural end, and this spirit permeates his entire view of *Adab* and of its place in the Islamic cultural tradition.

Chapter Five

ATTITUDES TOWARDS THE PAST

Historiography

This wide-ranging curiosity of Jāḥiẓ must, of course, be seen against its historical background: an Arab Muslim empire that sat astride the Eurasian land mass, linked from one end to another by a network of commercial routes and cities with large urban populations. As that empire expanded horizontally, its consciousness of time was to grow vertically as well. A sense of the great antiquity of the past was becoming apparent to educated Muslims of the eighth and ninth centuries, helping to deepen an already well-entrenched historical attitude inherited from the Koran and *Ḥadīth*. In addition, the problems of this cosmopolitan empire were such as to create a demand for guidance in all walks of life, both private and public. The development of historical writing in Islam is thus one place where the modern scholar can examine an important aspect of Islamic culture, namely the Muslim's view of his own place in the universe, his own historical self-image. What is the relationship of Islam historically to pre-Islamic civilizations? What is the true meaning of the Islamic past, present, and, indeed, future?

As we have seen, a historical impulse was found within Islamic revelation from the very beginning. The Koran, while not a history book, is obsessed with history. The *Ḥadīth*, both early and late, often amplifies the historical material in the Koran and in Muḥammad's own life. The early biographers of the Prophet set down his life in historical sequence in order to situate his whole prophetic experience in time and place and to facilitate the scholar's need for exact guidance and interpretation.

But parallel with this sacred interest in history, there was also a secular interest as well. We have already mentioned the interest shown by the Umayyads in antiquities of all kinds. This, however, was not mere antiquarianism but reflected a need for a historical self-image as well as guidance in affairs of state. The political struggles of the early community also acted as a powerful stimulus for historical writing, since many of Islam's earliest sects tried to justify their views by appealing to historical precedent. The party of ʿAlī in particular was very conscious of history since they differed from other Muslims on points that could only be settled by reference to history, and it is no accident, therefore, that Shīʿism of various shades and colors was popular among many of Islam's earliest historians.

All these factors (Koran, *Ḥadīth*, administrative guidance, sectarianism) acted as powerful inducements to historical writing in early Islam. But as with prose *Adab*, so with historiography, the earliest historical works survive, if at all, only in fragments quoted by later writers, for, here too, the Abbasid persecution was only too successful in eradicating the culture of their enemies, the Umayyads. The little we know about historical writing in the first century or so of Islam suggests, however, the existence of two parallel traditions, the one concentrating on the biography of the Prophet and the early history of the community, written in the spirit of *Ḥadīth*, the other concentrating on non-Islamic, perhaps largely Biblical or Ancient history, as well as on the exploits of various Arab tribes and on Arabian antiquities in general. We cannot pronounce with finality on this subject because we have so little evidence to judge from, but we can clearly discern both a secular and a sacred content in early Islamic historiography.

When historical writing emerges into the full light of day in the early Abbasid period (mid-to-late eighth century), the line between sacred and secular becomes even more apparent. *Ḥadīth* became increasingly more technical in the sense that it came to concentrate more than ever before on the sayings and doings of the Prophet and of his early companions. History, however, had cast its net wider, and this is perhaps best evident in biography, which, in the early ninth century, came to include biographies not simply of the pious members of the community but of a cross-section of the whole Muslim *umma*, of all who, in one way or another, had taken part in the political dramas of early Islam.

As with *Adab*, so with historiography, the expansion of the Muslim empire had brought it face to face with civilizations and nations as well as long historical traditions with which that empire had to come to terms. This encounter necessitated a new form as well as a new style of historical writing. The challenge to the Muslim *umma* posed by this cultural encounter forced the Muslim historian, as we have seen above, to try to locate the entire historical experience of the *umma* within the framework of the cultures to which he was now exposed. This is a challenge that every religion of salvation must sooner or later respond to: What is our relevance to world history? In answering this question, the historians of the ninth century may have been inspired by answers already given to it by the *adībs*. In the process, however, they were also to define the scope, method, and value of history itself.

Let us therefore begin with the scope. The history best known to these ninth-century historians was first the Persian and second the Biblical. Persian historical works were probably translated into Arabic as early as the eighth century, and Muslim historians were greatly impressed by the length of that history, which seemed to stretch all the way back to the creation of the world. The judgment of the tenth-century historian Ṭabarī is typical:

> Scholars of all nations agree that Kayūmarth is the ancestor of the Persians. They disagree whether he is also Adam, the ancestor of mankind, an opinion we have already cited, or whether he is someone else. . . . Therefore the dating of past history by reference to the reigns of their kings is clearer and more illuminating than the dating based upon the reigns of kings of other nations. For no nation that traces its ancestry to Adam is known to have possessed such continuous kingship or dynastic rule.

This body of ancient history, as transmitted in the works of Muslim historians, has not yet been thoroughly examined by modern scholars to determine how much of it is fact and how much myth. In any case, here was a long line of kings descended ultimately from a Persian Adam, and the Muslim historian had to come to terms with it. The Biblical material was already partially historicized, e.g., in The Book of Kings, and here, too, the Muslim historian had to come to terms with another ancient historical tradition. Other national histories, e.g., the Byzantine, were also known by the ninth century, but none of these histories had either the political prestige or the religious relevance of the Persian and Biblical materials.

One common solution to this historical dilemma was historical synchronization. The Muslim historian strove to incorporate all earlier histories into one synchronized account, forming the essential historical background to Islamic revelation. By synchronizing the Persian and Biblical materials, the Muslim historian was at once acknowledging the relevance of that history to his own and incorporating it into his own self-image of his past, formed largely by the Koranic world-view. In this manner, a place was found for Arabian, Persian, and Biblical antiquity as well as Islamic revelation in the scheme of world history. Through it all could be detected the guiding hand of God, pitting kingship against prophecy until God Himself becomes the only King and Muḥammad His last Prophet.

By the tenth century, the attention of Muslim historians had come to focus on seven ancient nations, who were believed to have shared the earth amongst themselves and to have laid down the foundations of human civilization. These seven were the Persians, Chaldeans, Greeks, Egyptians, Turks, Indians, and Chinese. Collectively, these nations had evolved the principles of the various sciences. Individually, they developed one particular art or skill to a high degree. All other nations, for instance the Franks of Western Europe, were thought to be uncouth and savage, possessing no history that was worth recording.

Turning next to the method, we see that as the Muslim historians began to cast their nets wider, and to take an active interest in the history of nations around them, the methodology of *Ḥadīth*, which had served so well in establishing the accuracy of prophetic reports, was now no longer relevant or even possible. Histories of course continued to be written using the *Ḥadīth* methodology of *isnād*. Ṭabarī, the major historian of the *Ḥadīth* school, wrote as follows in defense of his method:

> For knowledge of the reports of past ages or of present events comes down to those who did not witness them or live as contemporaries of them only through the reports of reporters and the transmission of transmitters, not through rational deduction or mental inference.

But *isnād* was frequently unavailable for such histories as Indian or Byzantine. Here the ninth- and tenth-century historians who dealt with such topics had to evolve rational criteria for testing the truth of reports. Such criteria were often adopted from their colleagues: the scientists, philosophers, or theologians who were at that time engaged in defining and redefining the methodology of scientific research or polemical argumentation. The scientist and polymath al-Bīrūnī (died after 1050), in contrast to Ṭabarī, summarizes the rational methodology to be employed in history and its relevance to continued scientific observation as follows:

> Those historical reports that conform to the limitations of possibility are to be treated as one treats true reports, provided there is no witness to the contrary. For we have observed and still observe natural phenomena the like of which, had they been reported as having occurred in an age earlier than our own, we would pronounce impossible.

Historian-scholars, in the spirit of Jāḥiẓ, were beginning to view history in terms of a scheme whereby man could be understood in natural and social terms. The style evolved was therefore to be matched to content: it was frequently a simple and continuous narrative, unencumbered by the *Ḥadīth* style because unencumbered by the horizons of *Ḥadīth*, and owing most, perhaps, to the *Adab* style of the period in which they wrote.

Finally, as regards the value of history, the historians of the ninth and tenth centuries had little difficulty in justifying their activity, especially when we bear in mind the great importance attached to history in the Koran. For one thing, history was the record of the encounter of God with man, and, by studying the history of that encounter, man could gain deeper knowledge of his relation to God. But there was also a humanistic value in the study of history. In studying the history of man, one gained a deeper understanding of human politics and society. Accordingly, many Muslim historians addressed themselves either directly or indirectly to the ruling circles of their times, who were often willing to benefit from the political "lessons" that history had to teach. Much of this history is political in nature, centering on political turmoil and on the sayings and doings of great men. History is a "mirror for princes," where the secret of political power could be learnt and employed to best advantage. Thus, the historian Miskawayhi (d. 1030) prunes history of everything but its major political events, which, he maintains, are likely to occur again in the future; he omits all miracles of prophets because they are of no practical value. His history, significantly entitled *The Experiences of Nations*, seeks to establish the true value of history: "of all people, those who stand to gain most value and benefit from it are those who have attained great prominence in life, such as viziers, army leaders and rulers of cities."

In a larger sense, history was also seen as a repository of human wisdom. It was here that historians made their contribution to the "great debate" of the ninth century, for many of them included in their histories lengthy introductions on the cultural history of ancient nations, quoting extensively from their wise men or philosophers on diverse topics of interest to the Muslim community. This is where the wisdom of the past was seen to be relevant to Islamic wisdom.

In all this activity, however, the historians of the ninth and tenth centuries did not lose sight of the practical, legal, and administrative needs of both the lawyers as well as the state secretaries of their society. For the benefit of both these groups, they evolved an annalistic and dynastic framework for easy reference when historical guidance was needed in public affairs or legal judgment. This annalistic-dynastic framework was adopted by Muslim historians down to modern times.

Not all these historians, of course, were equally interested in the theoretical implications of their subject. All of them, however, believed that history was neither haphazard nor accidental. A few speculated about the nature of historical truth and on the nature of cognition itself. These few, however, exercised an influence out of proportion to their number, and their speculations on the nature of historical enquiry culminated in Ibn Khaldūn. Let me summarize the views of two of these historians by way of conclusion to these remarks on classical Islamic historiography. The first of these, Yaʿqūbī (d. after 902) was the first Muslim historian to incorporate a sizeable body of ancient history and wisdom into his historical work; he thus popularized a type of world cultural history that was of considerable influence in later Muslim historiography. Yaʿqūbī provides detailed histories of the various sciences of his day, such as philosophy, astronomy, and medicine, and has much to say about ancient religions and chronologies. To be well grounded in any science, according to Yaʿqūbī, is to be grounded in its history and principles. The fact that he was also a noted geographer added depth and latitude of interpretation to his historical narrative. The patterns of political history are determined, for Yaʿqūbī, by the style of government and character of individual rulers, a reflection of his view of the intimacy of the relationship between governor and governed. Yaʿqūbī was aware of the role that the ruling classes played in shaping history, a view later to be elaborated by Ibn Khaldūn.

The second of these historians, Masʿūdī (d. 956), was a Twelver Shīʿite* with rationalist theological leanings. His wide ranging interest in all the sciences of his day led him first to produce works on these sciences, both religious and natural, and finally to cap his scholarly activity with a series of massive works on history, which he says he embarked upon only after he had satisfied his other scientific interests. History, for Masʿūdī, is not very unlike what it is for a present-day historicist:

> Were it not that scholars recorded their own ideas down the ages, the principles of knowledge and its ends would all be lost. For it is from history that every science is derived, every wisdom is deduced. . . . The superiority of history to all other sciences is self-evident and its honored status is accepted by all rational men. None can master it and gain certainty as to what it contains and how to receive and transmit it except one who has devoted himself totally to (the pursuit of) knowledge.

Patterns then begin to emerge, having to do with the rise and fall of kingdoms and nations, societies and cultures. Political decline, for Masʿūdī, is often the result of a disturbance in the social order caused by the injustice or greed of rulers. The reader of Masʿūdī may well speculate that this emphasis on justice as the primary social bond reflected the mood of new urban classes that were seeking justice in their social and economic relationships.

To determine truth in history, Masʿūdī frequently resorted to his own extensive knowledge of the sciences of his day, going far beyond Ṭabarī's somewhat timid view of history as accuracy of transmission. For Masʿūdī, accuracy in history meant the testing of historical reports against the accepted laws of natural phenomena, so that man is at all times seen and judged against his habitat and climate. Masʿūdī, however, remained attached to a view of a world dominated by a God who repeatedly manifests His presence by guiding the destiny of His creation. And whereas the world of Islam may be torn by chaos and fragmentation, knowledge itself, according to Masʿūdī, continues to advance from one era to the next, as if in obedience to some guiding principle of progress. Thus, classical Arabic Islamic historiography manifests a universality of historical interest that is, arguably, unique in medieval historiography as a whole. This interest extends not merely to the ascertaining of the high points of pre- and non-Islamic nations, but also to an awareness of the relativity of world cultures. By the tenth century, historiography had accumulated a great deal of information about other nations, ancient as well as contemporaneous, from China to Frankish Europe. From this evolved theories of what constitutes a nation. Language, territorial kingship, national laws and customs, climate, and geography were all topics of discussion.

From the viewpoint of the modern historian, classical Arabic Islamic historiography contains a very rich corpus of accurately ascertained facts. And while much of it relates to the sayings and doings of great men, there is also much material about populist movements and traditions. The classical historians no doubt reflected the concerns of their own scholarly class, and their attitude towards "commoners" was frequently one of contempt. These commoners, however, were not banished, either from their histories or from biographical dictionaries. From this, it is possible for the modern historian to reconstruct a vivid socioeconomic portrait of a major world civilization. This task has yet to begin in earnest.

Chapter Six

THE MYSTIC QUEST

Sufism

Sufism, or Islamic mysticism, is, of all the cultural products of Islamic civilization, perhaps the most difficult to define, classify, or categorize. One cannot easily say what it is because there is in Sufism a strong anti-intellectual spirit: indeed one might be tempted to call Sufism a malaise of the intellect. Nor can one easily classify the individual Sufis into movements or schools and categorize their teachings as monistic, pantheistic, and so forth, largely because the Sufis as a body inhabit a twilight zone between appearance and reality, illusion and truth. In fact, most of them claim to have transcended intellectual knowledge itself *(ᶜilm)* and to have attained a very special type of knowledge which they call gnosis *(maᶜrifa)*, making it difficult, if not impossible, for the student of Sufism to label their highly individualistic visions of God and man. Nevertheless, we must attempt to describe their experiences, however inadequate the result may be, simply because the Muslim Sufis themselves were, unlike the mystics of many religious traditions, very much concerned with the relevance of their experiences to the common man. If one were to seek a parallel with Christian movements, one might say that, on the whole, the Sufis were more like friars than monks. That is to say, their vision of God compelled them in the direction of public preaching and sermonizing rather than of monastic seclusion and retirement. Their experience of God was, for them, something to be shared with the rest of their community, even though they realized that not everyone could follow them along the Sufi path.

Let me begin, therefore, by attempting to describe what one might broadly term the Sufi mentality or the Sufi attitude of mind. To begin with, it would seem to me necessary to distinguish between the various historical stages and the various levels of meaning attendant upon the evolution of any universal religion of salvation, indeed of any ideological system. This means not only that the preoccupations of each generation of the faithful often differ in accordance with the different historical experiences they encounter, but also that the interpretation put upon that religion or ideology by succeeding generations can often differ radically, if not in content at least in mood, from the interpretation of their predecessors. In other words, not only does history itself bring forth new needs. These new needs are often expressed in new moods of religious experience and understanding demanding new interpretations of texts. As regards the Sufi movement itself, one might draw a fruitful parallel between certain aspects of that mood and the Romantic mood of early nineteenth-century Europe. Sufism, like Romanticism, represented a revolt against the formalism and intellectual dogmatism that seemed to them to dominate the lives of fellow religionists. Ritualism and reason were no longer adequate as expressions of the totality of religious experience. Also like Romanticism, the Sufi mood sought an outlet in a heightening and a quickening of the perception of Divine reality. This is why I attempt to analyze the literary imagery of the Sufis, for it is often in this imagery that one finds a way to unravel, and perhaps even to share, in the intensity of their religious experience.

So far, I have argued that the Sufi spirit shares common characteristics with other historical movements that rejected or transcended the legalistic intellectual rigor of their own traditions in the name of a more heightened experience of that tradition itself. Faith for the Sufis could not be a question of intellectual certainty. It was, rather, a question of ecstatic perception of reality that transcended rational conviction: unquestioningly more satisfying because it was a more immediate recognition of the reality of God. Ghazālī* (d. 1111), the famous twelfth-century Sufi, defined Sufism as a "knowledge of origins," a curious phrase until we realize that what is involved is a recapturing of a religious truth that has been, for too long, overburdened by intellectual constructions. To gain a knowledge of origins is to go behind, beyond, below the surface of religious life: to approach God not through the systematization of religious thought but through the investigation of the origin of religious thought itself; to seek God, not through the mediation of the intellect but through the recognition of what lies beyond the intellect. For the Sufi, it is in the experiences of the psyche rather than in rationalization that the direct encounter with God is to be sought. Turning to God, therefore, is in its earliest phases an act of will rather than a construct of the mind.

To underline this contrast between the psyche and the mind, the Sufis, as I will show below, frequently resorted to sensual imagery. This heightening of experience is represented in their imagery as a heightening or intensification of the sense of taste *(dhawq)*. For it is tasting that constitutes for them the most direct, the most intense sense experience of all. Tasting is the sum total, the quintessence of sense experience, the one in which the psyche partakes most fully in that which is to be experienced. To know God is to taste the joy of His presence, to partake in the ecstasy of the communion with Him.

This, in brief, is what one might call the Sufi mood. It is necessary, however, before we proceed to an analysis of Sufi imagery, to say something about the historical origins and development of Sufism and to situate it in time and space within Muslim culture as a whole, for I do not want to give the impression that Sufism was somehow a freakish or outlandish movement in Islam. By examining its origins and development, I hope to show that Islam, from its earliest days, contained within it the seeds of Sufi development. It is also important to remember that the Sufis from the beginning attached a very special importance to meditation upon the Koran and were some of its most interesting and attractive commentators.

When we discussed the Koran, I tried to show how immanent the presence of God was and how immediate the response of man could be, and must be, to the Divine reality. This immediacy of contact between the Muslim and his God precluded, from the beginning, the existence of any kind of personal or institutional mediation. All Muslims are spiritually equidistant from God because all Muslims have equal access to Him. At the same time, there is in the Koran an oft-expressed suspicion of monastic seclusion and a strong urge towards the fellowship of believers. All can draw near to God, and yet all must assume responsibility, direct or indirect, for the welfare of the community. According to a prophetic *Ḥadīth*, the mark of true piety is beneficial service to the community. Unlike the Christian asceticism of the Near East on the eve of Islam, with its strong emphasis on withdrawal from the world, Muslim piety commanded social involvement. To live with God is also to live with His creatures. Hence, Sufism from its earliest origins was deeply concerned with social ethics and with the exhortation to virtue. In all probability, their social origins are to be sought among the preachers and Koran-readers of the very early years of the Muslim community.

Etymologically, the word "Sufi" comes from the Arabic *ṣūf*, meaning undyed wool. It was used to describe the woolen garments of certain ascetic Muslims who, from the earliest period of Islam, were deeply disturbed by the political turmoil in which the Arab Muslim state was engulfed almost as soon as it was created. The woolen garment was perhaps a badge or a uniform used as a sign of protest against the immense luxury and wealth that the Islamic state came to possess as a result of its dramatic conquests in the Near East and Persia. The wearing of coarse wool was thus at once a mark of asceticism and of protest against what they felt to be the political and moral deterioration of the Islamic *umma*.

To asceticism, however, was added another dimension: the intensive meditation upon the Koran as part of a quest for its deeper meaning. These two dimensions, the ascetic protest and the deeper investigation of the Koranic text, were responsible for the rise of the Sufi movement. As we have already seen, the Koran lent itself to this sort of individual meditation by frequently exhorting the Muslim, not merely to contemplate the signs of God, but also to investigate his own inward experiences, "To hear what is being done to him," as Ibn al-ʿArabī* (d. 1240) put it. To the Sufis, both early and late, Muḥammad's Koranic revelations were themselves the result of mystical experiences, and in their attempt to recreate these experiences, many Sufis would utter pronouncements that were prophetic or oracular in nature. Indeed, as I shall show below, many were to find in verse the only adequate vehicle for the expression of their mystical utterances. By re-enacting within themselves the Prophetic experience, they often spoke like prophets and for this reason were to earn the suspicion or hostility of their fellow Muslims, especially in their early days. No one could claim to recreate the prophetic moment without simultaneously running the risk of being thought a pseudo-prophet. Centuries were to pass before the Sufis were accepted fully into the spectrum of Islamic religious life.

In the Koranic text itself, certain verses and chapters were especially precious to the Sufis because they seemed to them to capture the essence of mystical experience. Among these, none was more precious than the famous verses in the middle of the "Light" chapter, which give their name to the whole chapter and appear upon examination to be totally unrelated to their context. These verses, as we have seen elsewhere, describe the Light of God by comparing it to a lamp in a niche, perpetual and self-sufficient, an eternal flame fed by oil that shimmers and glows without need of fire: a light encapsulated eternally in the human breast. God's light is an inward dimension, to be sought through an inward psychic contemplation. It is something we can cherish and embrace, once we are aware of it, by the power of love. In order to do so, man must redirect, reorient his will, make himself receptive to this inner light, be in tune with the divine potential that makes its home in his heart. The heart, therefore, must be cleansed and "expanded" (Koran 94) and made to seek nothing but the light of God.

The Sufi encounter with God could lead, and often did lead, to the love of God. The early Meccan chapters of the Koran, however, especially those that describe Muḥammad's earliest revelatory experiences, emphasize the majesty of God and the awe *(hayba)* which this encounter inspired in him. If God is the God of compassion and beauty, inspiring love in the faithful, He is also the God of majesty and justice, thus fearful and awe-inspiring. In fact, it would seem that the early Sufis tended to emphasize the overpowering majesty of God more than His love. They saw Him as a being incommensurate with and incomparable to His creation. It was a later Sufi theorist, al-Hujwīrī* (d. 1072), who theorized that God's majesty and God's beauty were in fact two aspects of the same divine reality: the first leading us towards a sense of awe and the second towards a sense of fellowship. We, in turn, might theorize that the emphasis on God's majesty was the public or political aspect of Sufi preaching, whereas the emphasis on God's beauty was the individual or contemplative aspect: God as master and God as friend.

The ascetic behavior of the early Sufis and their intimate involvement with the masses gave them considerable popular appeal at a time when Muslim scholars as a body were turning their attention increasingly to system-building and legal-theological theorizing. By appealing directly to the masses and by rejecting indirectly the dogmatism and intellectualism of the *ʿulamāʾ*, or religious scholars, the Sufis were in effect challenging the emerging religious establishment on two fronts: the social as well as the intellectual. For both reasons, the early Sufis became suspect in the eyes of religious scholars. This early period has been called the heroic age of Sufism, the age when great Sufi masters or saints *(awliyāʾ)* often escaped with their lives only because of their mass following, who were perhaps more impressed by the style of their lives than by their cryptic and prophetic utterances. For, no matter how outwardly or inwardly respectful the Sufis were to the commandments of the law, there is in all mysticism an antinomian tendency, a tendency to transcend or rise above the law as the mystic approaches a direct and experiential knowledge of God. In some respects, the law or *sharīʿa* was to the Muslim Sufis what the Church was to the early Christian mystic: essential for a religious *community* but irrelevant for individual religious experience. This was the tragic conflict that Ḥallāj, the great Sufi master of the tenth century, was intent upon bringing to a head. In his life and, even more, in his death at the hands of his enemies, he marked the end of this first heroic period of Sufi development. By simultaneously challenging the literal requirements of the law (e.g., in his unorthodox interpretation of the rite of pilgrimage) and insisting on being punished according to the law, he intended his death to be a sacrificial act of love, a Christ-like gesture of dying for the sake of the law while affirming man's divine capability of rising above it.

Only a few Sufis were later on to suffer the same fate. The martyrdom of Ḥallāj shocked his contemporaries as well as his successors. From then onwards, one detects in the history of Sufism a tendency towards theorizing and systematization that they had hitherto shunned. It may, therefore, be possible to divide Sufi history into two periods, the first or heroic age of Sufi saints and the second period of discipline and compromise, the age of Sufi theorists. No doubt this distinction is oversimplified, but the transition to the later stage is best represented in the works of Ghazālī and Ibn al-ʿArabī as well as in the gradual evolution of the Sufi orders. The Sufis had always seen man as God's representative on earth, entrusted with the task of establishing a divine order. This to them was the moral of the story of Adam in the Koran. They had also seen man as possessing a divine dimension within himself, a dimension that he must investigate and come to terms with. Therefore, the need to recreate this order came with time to be institutionalized. Sufism, from about the eleventh century onwards, was becoming an educational process, and various Sufi orders organized around great teachers were springing up all over the Muslim world. With increasing institutionalization, the Sufi movement as a whole was beginning to draw closer to the *Sharīʿa* scholars and to their institutions. It is often said that Ghazālī was the man who effected a reconciliation between the Sufis and the religious scholars. But given the historical development of both in the direction of greater institutionalization, it is difficult to ascribe this synthesis to the work of one man, no matter how important his work may have been. In fact, the Sufis were to infiltrate into Muslim life through two channels: the *ribāṭ*, or frontier outpost of warriors leading a communal life of warrior saints, and the *madrasa*, or college of higher religious learning first established in the tenth century to combat Shīᶜite propaganda and later to become a potent instrument of state social policy and a training school for civil servants. By the fourteenth and fifteenth centuries, it was becoming normal for all religious scholars to be also members of Sufi orders, as one can discover by reference to the biographical dictionaries.

But Ghazālī and Ibn al- ᶜArabī were, of course, very important figures in the development of Sufism. The first was to offer Sufism as as vital spiritual dimension of life by pointing out that Sufism afforded man a measure of religious certainty that no intellectual proof could possibly furnish. Once man is plagued with doubt, once he falls victim to a devastating agnosticism, no amount of rationalization on the one hand or simple piety on the other can offer comfort. For the true and sincere agnostic, Sufism can provide a direct experience of the reality of God that can satisfy his deepest psychological and intellectual malaise, offering a spiritual therapy based upon intuitive rather than rational certainty. Ghazālī, however, did not remain on the Sufi heights, so to speak. His experience of Sufism was to lead him back to the foundations of Islam's various religious sciences, explaining, defending, and ordering each in turn, placing each in its proper relationship with the other, arguing for the necessity of every branch of learning by seeing it as part of a greater systematic whole. Ghazālī, therefore, belongs to the company of theorists rather than saints. Having traversed the whole gamut of Islamic sciences and having himself experienced a whole spectrum of psychological moods, he set out to create a vision of that whole, which he saw in terms of a hierarchical system that needs to cater to men of diverse intellectual and spiritual temperaments and needs. Within this system, Sufism occupied an honored place, but it did not by any means render the other religious sciences redundant, as earlier Sufi saints were sometimes tempted to claim. For Ghazālī, the encounter with Sufism lent his system spiritual intensity and immediacy, since Sufism gives man a taste of what religious life could become. Not everyone, however, can become a Sufi, and so ordinary men need to understand religious truth in terms of either the images and metaphors of the Koran or the logical and intellectual proofs provided by theology or the law.

Sufi awareness is a specially heightened form of religious experience which proceeds by exploring the inward dimensions of the law. The ways to God are many and diverse, and Sufism for Ghazālī serves to redirect and rededicate the soul towards God. But the soul cannot do so by setting itself up in opposition to the law. On the contrary, Ghazālī, if anything, reinforces the position of law as the formative foundation of religious life and practice. Sufism, however, is a window open to God and one that some Muslims can and should use to fortify, confirm, and revive their faith. Ghazālī relates the following parable:

> The difference between *ʿulamāʾ* and *awliyāʾ* is that the first acquire the sciences and bring them into the heart, while the Ṣufi *awliyāʾ* cleanse and polish the heart itself. The story goes that the Chinese and the Byzantines once boasted before a king about their skill in painting. The king decided to test their claims by providing a screen where the Chinese would decorate one side and the Byzantines the other. A curtain was placed between them so that neither side could see the other. The Byzantines collected together the most wonderful paints. The Chinese brought nothing, simply polishing their side. When the Byzantines were done, the Chinese said that they too were done. The king in surprise asked how they had finished without using any paints. Never mind, said the Chinese, just lift the curtain. When this was done, the wonder became visible. Through their side shimmered the Byzantine work of art but with added effulgence. Their side was more beautiful because it was more polished. The *ʿulamāʾ*, like the Byzantines, are concerned to acquire and inscribe the sciences, while the *awliyāʾ*, like the Chinese, polish their hearts. The heart of the man of faith dies not, nor does his knowledge vanish after death.

The other great Sufi theorist was the thirteenth-century Spanish Sufi Ibn al-ʿArabī, often called *al-shaykh al-akbar*, the Great Master. He was probably the most comprehensive and most influential of the Sufi thinkers of the post-Ghazālī period. By his time, Sufism had already developed a speculative system and had become central in Muslim thought. Sufi thinkers like Ghazālī had attempted to describe the whole universe from a Sufi point of view. This tendency was to be pushed even further after Ghazālī.

Ibn al-ʿArabī was a central figure in this movement towards what later on came to be known as the Illuminationist Philosophy *(al-Ḥikma al-Ishrāqiyya)*.

The system of Ibn al-ʿArabī was a fusion of many elements: literary, philosophical, and spiritual. The literary aspect was expressed in a symbolism of letters and numbers together with a large body of verse, much of it of exquisite beauty, where the whole universe is seen to mirror the light of God. God is the one true reality but His creation is a world of shadows. Therefore symbolism is essential to unravel the shadows in order to attain the reality beyond. The task of man is to polish the mirror of his soul so as to reflect the light of God. The world is then found to consist of a series of mirror images of God, an endless series of divine manifestations. The philosophical part of his system is more complex because the student recognizes within it elements of diverse philosophical schools: Neoplatonism, Aristotelianism, and pre-Socratic philosophy. The concept of the unicity of God and of His Absolute Being was derived from Plotinus, who also inspired Ibn al-ʿArabī's imagery of the emanation of light. Pythagoras, Parmenides, and Empedocles inspired his symbolism of letters and numbers as well as his views concerning the structure of the world, whether we wish to call it monistic or pantheistic. From Aristotle came the concept of the chain of being, which in Ibn al-ʿArabī's system appears as gradations of light. The whole is infused with a prophetic spirituality that describes the mind as a limiting factor (*ʿAql*: bridle) in the quest for God. To quote him: "It is not the mind that reconstructs, but rather the reconstruction that fills the mind." The mind itself is a passive receptacle, totally overshadowed by a God who cannot be circumscribed. Faith is a constant process of renewal, a constant recreation of the experience of prophets. It is the heart rather than the mind that is the locus of revelation in a world whose most characteristic movement is one of pulsation: towards God and away from Him. It is as if the whole universe, like the human heart, is constantly throbbing: contracting and expanding to accommodate a Divine Reality that embraces all opposites, a dialectical reality if you prefer, mirrored in microcosm in man himself.

I come, finally, to Sufi imagery. The problem here is to try to reconstruct the images that the Sufis used in their vivid but often baffling descriptions of the mystic vision of God. I have already alluded to their use of the metaphor of tasting to describe the partaking of man in the ecstacy of God's presence. Furthermore, many of them found it neccessary to put their thoughts down in verse, often without paying much attention to the rigid rules of Arabic prosody (which, incidentally, is one reason for the popularity of Sufi poetry among modern Arab poets), as if these fragments of verse were, consciously or otherwise, an emulation of Koranic revelation. In other words, they were reenacting, not only the experience of prophesy but also the style of the prophetic utterance, and some went so far as to "transmit" direct revelations from God. Ibn al-ʿArabī, for example, significantly called his great work *The Meccan Revelations.*

Let us now isolate a few of these dominant Sufi images and attempt to build a composite picture of their intricate world view. First and foremost, there is the image of light. This is the central image, not only because God is identified with the light, but also because man himself lives literally in the shadow of God. This theme is developed further in the Sufi image of man asleep and man awake, representing the Sufi emphasis upon continuous human awareness of God. The owl and the bat are frequent and popular Sufi images of a creature that stays awake when all the rest of God's creation are asleep. The light of God is said to be hidden behind a veil, an image already familiar from the Koran. The Sufis compared this veil to the veil that hides the radiant face of the beloved woman. The light, the veil that hides it, the constant awareness of it, the love that lies hidden beyond—these are the constituent elements of the "beatific vision" of the Sufis. By removing this veil, they enter into the imminent presence of God like lovers. They return to the pristine state of pure spirituality and, in the process, they undergo an "emptying of the self": a psychological transformation into a state of peace, intimacy, and comfort. Paradise itself becomes a present dimension.

Another dominant image is the image of the journey to God. Here, the model for the Sufis was Muḥammad's own journey to heaven, alluded to in the Koran and amplified with a wealth of detail in the *Ḥadīth*. Linked to this image of the journey are images of "ascent" and of "flight" as well as the frequent imagery of birds and moths. It is important to remember here that the Sufis conceived of their journey to God as taking place in stages, corresponding to continuous unravelling of different layers of religious meaning and experience. The Sufi way was not sudden, but rather a gradual and cumulative ascent to God. Like a moth circling ever closer to a flame or like a bird flying higher and higher in great spiral patterns, Sufi awareness may be called a centripetal force, each state drawing the Sufi closer and closer to the center.

To begin with, there is an experience of dissolution of the part in the whole, a state of pure spirituality and timelessness, compared by the thirteenth-century Sufi ʿAṭṭār* to the state of becoming at one with the Ocean of God, a loss of individuality in the identification with wholeness. It is the moment that, once attained, inspires constant longing for its renewal, a moment that stamps itself indelibly on the soul of the Sufi. This state of constant longing makes the Sufi peculiarly sensitive to God's creation, alive to the infinite spiritual potential of the human soul and eager that others like himself should also partake of that moment of union. That moment renders the Sufi an instrument of God, infusing his whole life with symbolic meaning, of which he is now fully aware, and returning him to his original state of selflessness. Eternity becomes a living dimension of life, not an abstract construction of the intellect. The image and the image-maker are finally united in love.

The God that the Sufi vision reveals is a God of tender mercy, comfort, and love—a God that renders all human preoccupations irrelevant and insignificant, infusing all creation with His light, a light that dispels all doubt, a light that makes all things intelligible. Constant spiritual exercise and discipline make this light a daily dimension of the life of the Sufi, so that wherever he turns, the light of God is reflected upon his surroundings. Ibn al-ʿArabī speaks of the helplessness of the Sufi, as if, when all other concerns have been set aside, the Sufi finds his whole being exclusively preoccupied with the Divine presence, his will so perfectly in harmony with God that all else is polytheism.

Chapter Seven

THE PLACE OF REASON

Theology

Prophets, it has been said, are not theologians. In the case of Islam, however, certain qualifications must be added. First of all, the Koran is filled with echoes of the theological debates of its historical environment, and it records the attacks of Islam's opponents upon it as well as Islam's answers to these attacks. In other words, Koranic theology is frequently polemical, stepping in to settle points of debate and to raise, in turn, questions and problems that were to dominate later Islamic theology. Secondly, as we have seen, Islam was born into a highly sophisticated theological environment; Christian theology especially had refined its theological weapons and represented a constant challenge to the new faith. Thirdly, the political turmoil of the early years of the Islamic community brought into focus a number of political attitudes or ideologies that in turn were to assume a theological coloring. Thus, the political and, by extension, the social and economic background of early Islamic society was a fertile breeding ground for early theological views. Even when these views later developed into highly abstruse intellectual systems, their political connotations were never very far from the surface. In fact, most Islamic political movements in the first three hundred years of Islamic history tended to have two wings: one being the militant wing and the other the "armchair" or theoretical. The first supplied the fighters in the field or city masses; the second supplied the theology or the intellectual weapons of the movement, thus helping to turn the movement into a sect.

The factors mentioned above make it difficult for us to reconstruct the historical origins of Islamic theology. It is likely that these origins must be sought in the Koran, in cultural encounters with non-Muslim religions and cultures, and in the political, social, and economic turmoil of the early Arab Islamic state. But all three factors were to stamp later Islamic theology with a highly polemical character, whether such polemics were directed at other Muslims or at non-Muslim groups. In general, however, one may distinguish two historical periods in the evolution of Islamic theology: the period of gestation, where the polemics and the basic themes were developed largely within an Islamic context, and the period of exposure, where the theologians began to use the tools of Hellenistic philosophy and the spectrum of topics dealt with widened to include the religious principles of Islamic life as a whole. Thus, from the political and intellectual in-fighting of the early Muslim community there arose in the eighth and ninth centuries a class of thinkers who believed that it was their special task to buttress the ramparts of Islam against heresy as well as external attack.

As we have seen, the towering political problem of Islam's first century of existence was the problem of legitimacy. It was a problem that was intimately bound up not only with the ethical question of who was best fit to rule but also with the social and economic dissatisfaction of segments of society that felt, rightly or wrongly, that they had been denied their fair share in the spoils of victory. A theology of political dissent, rooted in diverse interpretations of the Koranic text and in regional and tribal jealousies, served to divide the *umma* into two broad groups: those who wished to preserve its unity even as they recognized the political and ethical irregularity of its leaders and those who saw the *umma* as a community of "saints," rigorously excluding from its ranks those guilty of even minor sins. Within the two groups, there were wide variations of opinion, but it is important to remember that both groups conducted their struggle by claiming Koranic authority for their positions. The Koran has always been the major battlefield of Islamic theology.

Those who emphasized the unity of the *umma* styled themselves *ahl al-sunna waʾl jamāʿa* ("men of the right path and the community"), although little united them except their political quietism. Among them, however, the early *Ḥadīth* scholars, intimately associated with the merchants of the new cities, were to adopt the view that man's faith was a question that could only be resolved by God, that even major sins did not necessarily exclude a Muslim from the community, that good deeds, while important, were not a crucial part of faith, and that man's fate was predestined by God. The name *murjiʾa* ("postponers") was applied to one of the most active groups among them, the name itself being derived from their belief that man's faith was a question to be postponed and left up to God for ultimate decision. Politically, they represented those groups who, for various reasons, were trying to make their peace with the

Umayyad government. These were all positions that grew out of the turmoil of political struggle and were intimately connected with specific political and, indeed, economic crises.

Their opponents, the Kharijites, or seceders, were closely associated with the Arab tribal militias of the garrison towns and reflected political and economic dissatisfactions that in some cases antedated Islam itself. Their rallying cry was "No arbitration but God's," which, when translated into theological terms, meant a commonwealth ruled by the Koran and by men who would maintain the purest standards of ethical conduct. Major sins automatically excluded a man from the company of believers and consigned him to hell. The public performance of good deeds was to them an essential ingredient of faith, a quality that could increase or decrease depending on a man's works. Political leadership, therefore, belonged only to those most morally suited to assume its burdens—all other rulers were by definition usurpers. Despite the apparent "democracy" of their political view, their intimate connection with Arab tribalism made them unattractive to both city men and non-Arab Muslims. But the Kharijites, by their continuous revolts during Islam's first century of life, were to highlight ethics as a central issue of theological debate in early Islam.

No less activist than the Kharijites in this period were the Shīʿa, the party of ʿAlī, whose principal appeal in their early days was to lower-class urban groups. They, too, however, were not a coherent movement, but their most militant wing tended to be groups who brought into Islam ideas then generally considered extremist. These extreme Shīʿites, probably inspired by ancient Persian millenarian religions, attached quasi-divine qualities to the house of ʿAlī, pinning their hopes on various of his descendants and endowing them with superhuman powers of salvation and of mediation. Their metaphysics centered around a world view that considered the presence of such a semidivine figure *(imām)* to be an absolute prerequisite for the existence of the world, thus raising in an acute form the theological question of the relationship between God and His creation as another area of theological debate in early Islam.

These three groups, i.e., "the people of the community," the Kharijites and the Shīʿites, were, through their conflicts, to bring to the fore a number of political problems and directly or indirectly to articulate them in theological terms. The ethical problems of government were to raise a host of derivative problems like free will and predestination, the status of the sinner and the true definition of faith, while the Shīᶜites introduced a metaphysical dimension to theology that was later to inspire debates about the status of prophecy and the question of Divine creation. This period of gestation was to end in the early eighth century, for it was then that the basic societal institutions of the new Islamic state began to take shape.

A generation of relative peace in the middle Umayyad period (roughly A.D. 700-740) afforded the scholars of the cities of Ḥijāz, Syria, and Iraq the time and leisure to reflect upon the earlier turmoil and to define more systematically the theoretical foundations of their respective theological views. The majority of religious scholars had concluded some sort of peace with the political regime and thus were turning their attention increasingly to the problems of the organization of religious life within, not outside, the community. Foremost among these problems was the question of God's justice, debated most intensely among circles that were intimately involved in obtaining economic and social justice in their own urban environment. It is in this period also that one detects a greater degree of exposure to non-Islamic cultural and religious influences, hitherto largely ignored in the period of gestation.

The fundamental problems of Islamic theology were already laid down, therefore, when this second period began. Among the most influential movements that were to refine their theological principles in this period were the group known as the Muᶜtazila, who were to exercise a preponderant influence on the development of all later Muslim theology right down to modern times. The range of problems they dealt with as well as their polemical skills assured them a central place in Islamic theology to the point where it is no exaggeration to assert that all later Islamic theology has been, directly or indirectly, a commentary on Muᶜtazilism.

The accepted view of the origin of the word "Muᶜtazila" is that it refers to groups who refrained from taking part in the first civil war in Islam. The term *iᶜtizāl* refers to neutrality in political disputes. This neutrality was later elaborated in one of the earliest theses, which concerned the ethical status of a Muslim who had committed a major sin. According to the Muᶜtazilites, he was neither an unbeliever (the Kharijite thesis) nor a believer (the Murjiʾa thesis) but a transgressor *(fāsiq)*, one who commits a breach of contract and therefore, by extension, a person who occupied an intermediate ethical position. From this obscure and rationalist starting point, the Mu^ctazila were to develop into a quasi-political and intellectual movement, which, by the first quarter of the eighth century, succeeded in formulating its own creed under the heading of five main theses. These five theses were to remain the distinguishing characteristics of the movement for the rest of its life, although they were later elaborated by succeeding generations of theologians under the impact of Hellenistic philosophy during what I have called the age of exposure. By examining these five theses we would obtain an overview, not only of Mu^ctazilite theology, but also of the range of topics that Islamic theology as a whole was now embarking upon. I shall rearrange the usual order of these theses, beginning with the two predominantly ethical ones and going on to the three metaphysical ones.

1. *The intermediate stage (al-manzila bayn al-manzilatayn):* For the early Mu^ctazilites, the attempt to apportion praise or blame for the public acts of the main participants in the first civil war (656-661) was a pointless one. For them it was sufficient to assert that none of the Companions of the Prophet could be said to be a "transgressor," i.e., to be in an intermediate position. Rather, the main problem was ethical: what to do with the grave sinner? For these early Mu^ctazilites, a person could be a Muslim even though his grave sins temporarily made him a non-believer. In other words, faith was a changing quality depending upon rational knowledge of God's commandments. Grave sins therefore suspend this faith but do not negate it. The only sin that negates faith is a conscious and rational belief in polytheism. As a result, Mu^ctazilites were to define faith in terms of knowledge and reason. It was an intermediate definition between those who believed that faith could be wiped out by sin and those who believed that it was a constant quality implanted in man by God.

2. *Encouragement to the good and prohibition of reprehensible action (al-amr bi'l ma^crūf wa^cl nahy ^can al-munkar)*: This was the public aspect of Mu^ctazilites preaching, an ethical principle derived from repeated Koranic injunctions to establish the virtuous community and stress the public responsibilities of the individual believer. The Mu^ctazilites pursued this aim with vigor, and while later Mu^ctazilites tended to exaggerate the political role of their predecessors, it nonetheless appears that they exercised some influence on political life, especially in the later Umayyad and early Abbasid period (mid-

eighth century). In the early ninth century, when for a brief period, Muʿtazilism became the favorite dogma of the Abbasid caliphs, bands of them would roam the streets of Iraqi cities, admonishing the crowds and endeavoring to maintain public morals, while the intellectuals among them strove to dominate the judiciary corps and to engage in debate with both Muslim and non-Muslim opponents. Socially speaking, many of them appear to have belonged to the upper strata of urban craftsmen (e.g., perfumers, booksellers), and we find frequent comparisons in their writings between good works and honesty in commercial dealings.

The three remaining theses are all related to God. Here, the rational aspect of their creed may be seen most clearly. Once these are analyzed, however, one may legitimately ask why the Muʿtazilites adopted this rational theology and what were its later consequences.

1. *The Unity of God (Tawḥīd)*: The monotheism of the Muʿtazilites was of the strictest and most logically rigorous kind. God is above time and place, above all change and is in no wise corporeal. How, then, is one to interpret or understand the multitude of attributes with which God is described in the Koran? And, more pertinently, how is one to explain the passages in the Koran where God is said to possess such human attributes as eyes, hands, and so forth? In answer, the Muʿtazilites held that to call God "merciful" is not to ascribe mercy to him in an additive sense. To do so would be to set up a sort of pantheon of ideas and forms existing alongside God. Some of these attributes (e.g., life, knowledge) belong to the essence of God: they are not, by themselves, God nor are they other than God. These they called "attributes of essence." But God had another set of attributes, which relate to Him without affecting His essence, such as His will, speech, sight, and so forth. These they called "attributes of act," because they relate to His activity as Creator but do not subsist in Him. This led the Muʿtazilites to argue that the Koran was the speech of God and therefore created. It led them also to deny that God could ever be seen by the senses. The mind proves His existence with certainty, but there can be no sensory perception of Him. Therefore, all such Koranic passages that describe God as corporeal are to be interpreted figuratively. Human reason shows Him to be One and totally unlike His creation.

2. *The Justice of God (ʿAdl)*: The wisdom and goodness of God dictate His justice. This justice is manifest in His creation, which is wholly rational and intelligible. His goodness can admit no evil.

Sin and injustice can in no wise be ascribed to Him but only to His creatures, who, because of God's justice, are endowed with the power to act. Once this power is given, man becomes a sort of "second creator" and is fully responsible for both the good and the evil that he engenders. Man's freedom is, therefore, a logical consequence of the justice of God, for without this freedom man cannot be held responsible for his actions, and the whole scheme of the universe would become arbitrary and irrational. All religious laws, all good and evil, can be deduced by reason. Accordingly, there can be no inherent contradiction between reason and revelation. What God does aims at what is best for His creation: hence, revelation confirms His goodness and mercy and confirms also man's freedom and reason.

3. *Promise of paradise and threat of damnation (al waᶜd waʾl waᶜīd)*: This was a subsidiary thesis, directly dependent upon the justice of God and meant to emphasize the irreversible consequences of human action in the life hereafter. Many Muᶜtazilities, therefore, denied the possibility of intercession of the Prophet, a commonly held belief among certain pious circles. The faithful will assuredly be rewarded in paradise, and the unrepentant sinner will assuredly be damned in hell. To believe in intercession is to believe in an unjust and arbitrary God.

These are the five theses of the Muᶜtazilites. But in addition to them, the later Muᶜtazilites especially were to engage in lengthy controversies in the course of which theology itself came to be called *kalām* (polemical discourse). They left their imprint upon subjects that one normally does not associate with theology: e.g., politics, law, history, and even aspects of physics, such as atoms, motion, and so forth, especially those that could serve to explain the nature of human action. In the course of this, *kalām* became proverbial for its obscurity and was often regarded as useless and even dangerous by its opponents. Running throughout this theological web was the great struggle between an arbitrary world view and a rational world view, between a God and a Nature ultimately comprehensible to human reason and a God and a Nature that are ultimately incomprehensible; between the view that the human mind possesses the capacity to distinguish between what is intrinsically good and evil and a human mind which needs prophecy and revelation to spell out sin and its punishment. All these questions were brought to a head by the Muᶜtazilites.

Of all theological movements, the Muᶜtazilites were the ones who sought most actively to combat magic and superstition. To argue for a rational world view was also to argue against a magician: God who played with His creation, producing miracles and reversals of natural order. Furthermore, the connection between Muᶜtazilism and the urban craftsmen seems to have been a close one, and it is Iraqi urban decline in the late ninth and tenth centuries that explains the decline in their activities rather than the intellectual triumph of their adversaries, for we see them thriving again in the new and prosperous urban-based dynasties of north and west Persia in the tenth and eleventh centuries.

However, their theological adversaries did present them with a number of intellectual problems raised by their rigorous rationalism. In the course of these controversies, the Muᶜtazilites and their opponents were to leave their imprint on each other. Many later Muᶜtazilites of the tenth century, for example, were to recognize the logical difficulties in certain theological positions, e.g., how to explain the suffering of children. At the same time, their opponents were to recognize that the simplistic faith of some *Ḥadīth* scholars who insisted upon accepting the literal meaning of the Koranic text "without asking how" was inadequate and rationally unsatisfactory. The great opponent of the Muᶜtazilites was Ashᶜarī* (d. 935) and his school, a school that came to dominate Sunnite theology until modern times.

Was Ashᶜarī a mere follower of the anti-theological *Ḥadīth* scholar Ibn Ḥanbal* or was he more? It was clear that his own involvement in theology went quite contrary to the teachings of the master he professed to follow. In fact, the whole development of Ashᶜarī and of his school was a process of interaction between them and the Muᶜtazilites. Ashᶜarī's later followers spoke of him as the author of a synthesis between the two extreme positions: those who divested God of all attributes and those who ascribed human attributes to Him. Ashᶜarī spoke of "lifting God above" such discussions—of purifying Him from both attitudes. The Ḥanbalites, who were by then the leading anti-theological school, maintained that God's corporeality is to be accepted "without asking how," i.e., without further discussion. Ashᶜarī, however, maintained that we accept it "without knowing how," i.e., recognizing that such questions are beyond human reason. Again, God's speech and God's will are both attributes of essence, and God's speech is eternal even though the letters of the Koran are created. Good and evil are known only by revelation. Since

God's will is eternal, God is the efficient cause of all motion, including man's actions. To explain the resultant predestination, Ashʿarī and his school developed the doctrine of acquisition, where God creates the power in man and man "acquires" that power, since the act and the power to act happen simultaneously.

In all these views, Ashʿarī was intent upon demonstrating the essential limitations of human reason. Undoubtedly, a great many of his arguments as well as his methods were derived directly from the Muʿtazilites who dominated the horizons of his theology as well as those of his followers. Later Islamic theology was equally synthetical and eclectic and increasingly open not just to Muʿtazilism, but also to philosophical and mystical influence, as with Ghazālī. But theology was gradually to lose what little popularity it enjoyed over the course of centuries and to give way steadily to the law and to Sufism.

Philosophy

From a historical point of view, this part of Islamic culture is quite clearly the product of the impact of Hellenistic philosophy, more specifically of Plato, Aristotle, and Plotinus, on Islam. While the Indian and Persian heritage was of crucial importance in science, literature, and political thought, it did not contribute much to the rise of Muslim philosophy (*falsafa*).

The Muslim philosophers were, at all times, a tiny minority in Islam. They themselves tended to keep aloof from their scholar-colleagues, and these latter often regarded them as at best useless and at worst dangerous. Part of the reason for their aloofness was that they believed that philosophy could not be harnessed in the defense of religion as easily as theology. The philosophers on the whole adopted a negative attitude to theology because theology, in their eyes, vulgarized, misunderstood, and misrepresented certain basic philosophical concepts. Some were prepared to grant theology a slightly more useful function—that of defending the faith. To jurisprudence, they adopted a more favorable attitude because they recognized the importance of law as a force making for social cohesion.

Their colleagues, on the other hand, generally distrusted their activities either because 1) they distrusted the whole process of Hellenization as inimical to Islam, or 2) they believed that any contribution philosophy could make was already found in religion itself or in some other auxiliary discipline, e.g., philology. An interesting illustration of this is the fully preserved debate dating back from the early years of the tenth century between a philologist and a logician, where the philologist points out to the logician that whatever value there is in logic is already found in grammar and is, therefore, redundant. The fact that this particular logician was a Christian is noteworthy, because the hostility to philosophy may also have stemmed from its intersectarian character, it being a discipline to which Christians, Jews, and Muslims freely contributed.

Let me summarize very briefly those principles or views of philosophy that form the common stock of opinions held by most or all the Muslim philosophers from Kindī* in the ninth century to Fārābī* in the tenth century to Ibn Sīnā* (Avicenna) and Ibn Rushd* (Averroes) in the eleventh and twelfth centuries. First, they all believed that philosophy was a system of knowledge that must be mastered in the proper sequence and requires years of study. Therefore, its results or conclusions could not be applied haphazardly and out of context to fortify conclusions from other disciplines. Second, as an independent system of knowledge, philosophy is distinguished from all other systems by the fact that it can offer certain proof. Its methodology is called "demonstration" *(burhān)* as opposed to the rhetorical methodology of poetry or the dialectical methodology of theology. To master demonstration, one must begin with mathematics, then proceed through the various philosophic sciences such as logic, ethics, and politics until one finally arrives at metaphysics, the highest of them all.

Thus far, Islamic *falsafa* may seem indistinguishable from Greek philosophy. But the problems of Islamic philosophy were also very peculiar to itself and were never faced by a Greek philosopher. These problems may be summarized in one question: What is the role of philosophy in a society ruled by revelation, by a revealed law? Derivatively, what is the relationship between the philosopher and the prophet, between philosophy as a system of knowledge and religion as a system of knowledge? These were the questions to which Muslim philosophers applied themselves most insistently. They had to justify the existence of their discipline in, and to, their societies. Thus, in a society based on revealed law, the place of a jurist or a *Ḥadīth* scholar, a philologist or a Koran commentator, a historian or even a theologian was assured, indeed self-evident. But what is the place of a philosopher?

Some philosophers, like Kindī, believed that the highest truths of philosophy were in essential agreement with the highest truths of religion. But whereas religion proceeds by persuasion, rhetoric, and allegory so as to reach the masses, philosophy proceeds by demonstration, which alone can satisfy the few, the intelligentsia, who need demonstrative proof. Fārābī went further. He argued that the highest principles of religion were "derived from" philosophy, that philosophy establishes the ultimate truth, whereas religion, as he defines it, is "opinions and acts decreed and limited by conditions that are set for the group by their first leader." These opinions and acts are derived from philosophy. They teach concretely what philosophy teaches abstractly. Both are neccessary for the community, but philosophy remains supreme. Such opinions had to be expressed with a great deal of caution, and this is why Fārābī's writing is frequently of extreme complexity. It often placed him beyond the pale. Thus, for example, there is little doubt that he held, with Aristotle, that the world was eternal, having no begining and no end. This went clearly against the teaching of Islam (as well as Judaism and Christianity).

The sharpest attack on philosophy came from Ghazālī, a seminal figure in Muslim Sufism and theology. Ghazālī was to argue that certain branches of philosophy (e.g., mathematics, logic, ethics) could be tolerated by the Muslim community, provided one were not to expect the same kind of proof from religion, which because of its nature cannot provide such rigor. Such philosophical disciplines were to be "handled with care" lest they lead to unbelief. Ghazālī, however, quite rightly detected in metaphysical philosophy certain concepts (e.g., the eternity of the world) that were to him clearly antireligious and thus highly dangerous to the spiritual well-being of the Islamic community. Such opinions were to be exposed and combated with vigor.

Ghazālī's attack on philosophers drew a sharp rebuke from Averroes (d. 1198), who argued that the study of philosophy was in fact commanded by law since philosophy is the "science of last things" and the law commanded this study. Averroes maintained that the mistakes of philosophers were accidental and extrinsic to their discipline. Such mistakes in no way invalidated the study of philosophy. Being himself a judge, he was able to bolster his arguments with *Ḥadīth* and legal argument, combining in his person the two disciplines historically most antithetical to each other in

Islamic history. For he would argue that there are three ways to truth: demonstrative, dialectical, and rhetorical. The highest is demonstrative. If scripture conflicts with this, then one must reinterpret scripture because philosophy and religion do not disagree. Only the elite should take charge of this work of interpretation. For the mob to interpret the Koran is unbelief, and to vulgarize philosophy, as Ghazālī did, is to confuse the various ways to truth. Only those intellectually qualified should have accesss to demonstrative books. In other words, philosophy must be removed from the marketplace and must become the exclusive preserve of a small company of intellectuals. For the rest of society, divine law was a perfectly adequate guide to the good life, and if theology is to be practised at all, it must strictly adhere to its own methodology and must not venture into philosophical territory.

The finality of this answer has led many modern European students of Islamic philosophy to see in Averroes the last of the Muslim philosophers, the end of the line. In reality, however, Averroes was the last Muslim philosopher whose philosophy was found to be relevant to the development of European philosophy. Meanwhile, the Islamic tradition of philosophy was to survive for several centuries. The fact that this later, post-Averroes period is far less studied than the pre-Averroes period may also explain this outdated Euro-centered view that Islamic philosophy ends with Averroes. Averroes may have been the last of the great Muslim Aristotelians, but he was by no means the last of the Muslim philosophers.

The later course that Islamic philosophy was to take cannot be discussed at length here, and only its main outlines will be set forth. The path it followed was to bring it even closer to Sufism, which later was to dominate Islamic intellectual life. The origins of this drift towards mysticism were already present in the form of references scattered here and there in the writings of Fārābī, and especially of Avicenna, on the subject of the soul. As the philosophic soul attempts to attain its ultimate state of perfection, it strives, according to Avicenna, to love that perfection—a love of such intensity that Avicenna identifies it with the Sufi ideal.

Accordingly, the stage was set in the writings of later Muslim philosophers for what came to be known as the "Wisdom of Illumination," where the theoretical investigations of philosophy are used to arrive at the ultimate Sufi truths. This "new" philosophy claimed to represent a return to the pure foundations of philosophy itself, a revival of the mystical wisdom of Empedocles, Pythagoras, and Plato, who is seen as the first mystic. God, according to this new wisdom of illumination, is called the "light of lights," and His relationship to the world is one of a hierarchy of lights emanating from Him, while the souls of men become pure lights striving to return to the realm of Light. The well-known categories of philosophy such as matter and form, substance and accident, are said to be mere gradations of light and darkness. The Illuminationists claimed that they had not only "solved" the problems of philosophy but they had also discovered the true spiritual significance of all religions.

Chapter Eight

THE WORLD OF NATURE

Science

The Muslims of the classical period freely acknowledged that their scientific knowledge had its roots in the cultures of Babylonia, ancient Egypt, India, Persia, and Greece. Many Muslim scientists believed that science was as old as the world. In their eyes, this appeared to reinforce the Koranic belief that nature manifests itself in the handiwork of God.

Alchemy, astrology, and medicine were the earliest sciences cultivated by the Muslim Arabs. Alchemy is associated with the name of Khālid ibn Yazīd, an Umayyad prince, who is said to have learned its secrets from the Greeks. This science, which probably originated among ancient Near Eastern and Greek craftsmen, was, throughout its history in Islam, closely linked to the attempt at the transmutation of metals, especially baser metals into gold. Alchemy was therefore the science of the marketplace, holding the secrets of untold riches. Since all metals could in theory be turned into vapor, the task of the alchemist was to find the process of distillation that would recombine these vapors into purer metals. The search, however, was not confined solely to gold; other valuable substances, like perfume, could also be produced synthetically. Thus, the failure of alchemy to produce gold did not immediately decrease its popularity, since its methods could be applied to a wide variety of substances of commercial or medical value.

The fact that alchemy was one of the earliest sciences to be cultivated by Arab Muslims had important theoretical implications for the development of Islamic science in later periods. Alchemy, as received and developed by the Muslims, was based on the assumption that matter in the universe was in a state of balance. The four basic constituents of matter—earth, water, air, and fire—were characterized by four basic natures or qualities: dry, humid, cold, and hot. Greek science had already made this "discovery." The Muslim alchemists of the early period were to refine this theory by observation and experimentation and thus to introduce into Islam a theme that underlies much of later scientific speculation: the theme of reason versus experimentation, the universal versus the particular, *a priorism* versus empiricism, deduction versus induction, the presumed regularity or balance of the universe versus the observations that either confirmed or denied such regularity. Nor was this debate far removed from the theological concerns of the early Islamic community, since early theology, too, was intent upon detecting a divine order in the cosmos.

In the eighth and ninth centuries, medicine and astrology penetrated the Islamic world through a vigorous translation movement actively aided by the patronage of ruling circles. Indian, Persian, and Greek works of science were eagerly studied by a society that recognized their immediate practical value. From India, the Muslims learned about cycles and conjunctions, the influence that the heavenly bodies exerted on the sublunary world. In medicine, the school of Jundaysābūr, in southeast Persia, which had preserved and developed Greek medicine in an ancient Oriental environment, supplied the Abbasid court with its earliest and most renowned physicians. Both astrology and medicine served to popularize the view that man was in fact a physical microcosm living in a larger and more embracing macrocosm, a view that could with relative ease be harmonized with religious teaching about man's place in the universe of God. Thus, al-Kindī,

> This is why man. . . has been called a microcosm, for in him are found all powers present in the macrocosm, such as the powers of growth, of animal life, and of speech. In him is found the element earth such as bones and similar matter, the element water like the wet substances, the veins. . . the stomach, the bladder, and so forth as well as minerals and gum-like substances like brain and nerves. The inside of his stomach and all his entrails are like air. His innate heat is like fire. His hair is like plants. Parasites inside and outside him are like fauna. Every phenomenon that takes place in the sublunary region such as rain, thunder, winds, fissures, earthquakes, and so forth has its equivalent in man.

This did not, however, mean that these scientists, especially the alchemists and the astrologers, found ready acceptance among the larger body of religious scholars. These latter often suspected them of dabbling in magic, and the Koran itself was explicit in its condemnation of magic and star worship. Another cause for suspicion was the fact that many of the early transmitters of these two sciences were Christian monks, Magians, and Jews, who were thought to be attempting to corrupt Islam with the same occult sciences that had already led their own religious astray. The hostility to these sciences is reflected in several *Ḥadīths* that warn against alchemy and astrology, which are said to engender heresy, stupidity, and poverty. Not surprisingly, therefore, the lives and works of the earliest alchemists such as Khālid and the famous Jābir* are enmeshed in legend. The Jābir corpus of alchemy especially is associated with esoteric Muslim sects like the Ismāᶜīlis,* who were receptive to the occult sciences and to the world of symbolism upon which these sciences were based.

However, astrology, and to an even greater extent medicine, had powerful patrons in Islamic society and thus made a great impact on the progress of Islamic science as a whole. This impact was furthered when, in the course of the ninth century, the Greek philosophical corpus, which included the natural sciences, was translated into Arabic with the active encouragement of the Abbasid court. Islamic science now came into its own, vigorously asserting its right to a legitimate place in the Islamic curriculum. Many of the practitioners of astrology and medicine continued to be non-Muslims, but the theoretical foundations of these two, as well as other, sciences were of consuming interest to an ever wider circle of Muslim men of letters, historians, theologians, as well as scientists. Astronomy and meteorology, with arithmetic and geometry, were brought in to refine the method and foundations of astrology, while medicine was bolstered by growing experimentation in the field of physics, pharmacology, and zoology. The theoretical problems raised by research into these fields of science were vigorously debated in intellectual circles that were not scientific, despite the attempts made by the Muslim philosophers to arrogate to themselves the privilege of "overseers" and to claim that these sciences were inseparable from *falsafa*. Science, and more particularly scientific theories, were a free-for-all: the modern notion of specialization was foreign to the all-pervading theory of *Adab*, and acquaintance with scientific theory was soon held to be part of the total education of the *adīb*.

This process of assimilation was furthered by the fact that certain sciences were now clearly demonstrating their relevance to other branches of Islamic learning. The astronomers used their tables to establish more accurate dating of events and of Muslim prayer times, thus making their research more meaningful to historians and legal scholars. Physics, geometry, and arithmetic introduced new refinements into such concepts as motion, time, and place and thus helped to refine the argumentation of theologians who were intent upon analyzing the constituent elements of human action. Medicine fostered the view that man could be understood only against his physical and climatic background, which helped to link him even further to the larger world of creation. The emphasis on ritual purity in the Koran and *Ḥadīth* was frequently cited by medical authors as a justification of their activity.

I will not touch upon the actual contributions of Islamic science as such but will deal briefly with three themes that pertain to the place of science in general within classical Islamic culture. The first theme is the history of science as related by Muslim scholars. The second is the question of scientific method as understood and debated within the classical Islamic context. The third is the problem of scientific progress and the views expressed on this topic by various Muslim thinkers. In other words, an attempt will be made to analyze the Islamic views of the past, present, and future of science, as these views developed in the classical period.

As regards the origins of science, it was a widely-held belief in the period from the ninth to the eleventh centuries that almost all ancient nations had developed a body of scientific wisdom, a wisdom that "migrated" from one region of the earth to another until it found a final home in Islam. Pythagoras, for example, was said to have learned wisdom from the companions of King Solomon and geometry from the ancient Egyptians and then to have carried back this knowledge with him to Greece from whence it descended to the Arabs. A common point of debate among Muslim scholars was the question of the original home of wisdom. India and Greece vied for this honor, the most common view being that while India may have been the first home of wisdom, the Greek contribution to science was more lasting and more intellectually satisfying. Only the Chinese and the Turks were said to have been deficient in theoretical wisdom, although Chinese craftsmanship and technology were admired. This admiration for ancient wisdom was sometimes excessive, especially when it centered around men like Aristotle or Ptolemy, whose works were considered by many Muslim thinkers to be definitive. Muslim philosophers wanted to show that the sciences were in essence a Greek achievement whereas historians and men of letters would argue that they had an older lineage. Both groups, however, agreed that Islam had "inherited" these sciences, unlike Christianity, which was said to have nearly succeeded in snuffing out the sciences in the lands over which it ruled. Both also recognized that the sciences had a chequered historical career, rising and falling in accordance with the nations and lands that practiced them.

As regards scientific method, this was a field to which philosophers and theologians, as well as scientists, contributed. The central problem here was the scheme of knowledge itself and the place of scientific method within that scheme. The Muslim philosophers, following the Greeks, had divided the natural sciences into two: the theoretical and the practical. The theoretical sciences were said to be higher than the practical, in the sense that they provided the abstract or conceptual foundations upon which the practical or concrete sciences were based. Thus, for example, arithmetic and geometry were said to be higher or purer than astronomy because the latter derived its principles from the former. Apprehension itself was commonly said to have three ways or modes: the first was apprehension by primary knowledge; the second was apprehension by the senses; and the third was apprehension by investigation and inquiry.

The first mode, apprehension by primary knowledge, is what may be called the apprehension of basic or self-evident truths of logic or mathematics, which any person with any degree of rationality must immediately recognize to be so, e.g., that two is more than one, that a created thing needs a creator, and so forth. The second mode is what we would call apprehension by sense perception, i.e., knowledge derived from the senses. The third mode, apprehension by investigation and inquiry, includes what we would call empirical as well as rational, i.e., deductive apprehension. The debates which raged about these modes of apprehension were by no means confined to scientific circles, since theologians and philosophers, in particular, and also certain historians and men of letters, were deeply interested in the various theories of knowledge because of their implications for their own views of God, nature, and man.

The natural scientists tended to concentrate on the third mode of apprehension and to draw a distinction between research on the one hand and rational inquiry on the other. Medicine was a particularly popular field in which these theories of knowledge were tested out. Was medicine an essentially rational activity where the mind of man deduces and makes analogies from certain fixed principles, i.e., was medicine essentially like geometry? Or was it a field where research constantly brought forth new facts from the examination of particular cases, which were then subject to experimentation leading to new theories? Or was it in fact a combination of both, i.e., of *a priorism* as well as empiricism? The emphasis on experimentation was particularly prevalent among scientists, who believed in a steady increase in knowledge and were ready to challenge the authority of even the most respected ancient philosophers like Aristotle. It was also prevalent among those scientists who refused to conform to metaphysical or teleological theories that claimed to give the final account of the structure of the natural world. By rejecting what they called "imitation," they were asserting their belief that knowledge was essentially acquired through accumulation of experiences and were, consequently, asserting that knowledge itself is endless.

The belief in the endless progress of knowledge was in all likelihood inspired by the Islamic scientists, although the implications of this belief were taken up and developed by other thinkers who were not themselves practicing scientists. The belief in progress may also be related to the social and economic conditions prevalent in the Abbasid empire of the late eighth and early ninth centuries. It was by then an empire that had reached its greatest geographical extent. Its political triumph over its enemies gave many of its scholars a sense of unbounded confidence in their own intellectual superiority. A plentiful supply of paper enabled scholars to produce far more works than ever before. A network of commercial routes facilitated the meeting of Muslim scholars from distant lands. Finally, the patronage of the court and the growing institutionalization of scholarship itself in the judiciary corps provided the scholars with the material means necessary to pursue their research. All these factors encouraged Muslim scholars of a philosophical or scientific bent of mind to believe in a continuous advance of knowledge as between past, present, and future.

Jāḥiẓ was probably the first Muslim thinker to formulate a coherent theory of scientific progress, even though he was not a practicing scientist. His belief in the progress of knowledge derives from his own theory of how knowledge occurs in man. As we have seen already, Jāḥiẓ asserts that a human being learns in much the same manner as other animals, i.e., by the repetition of experience until enough experience is accumulated to permit discrimination. Accordingly, experience precedes rationalization and is in fact a prerequisite for it. This theory of knowledge gives prominence to the accumulation of experience, to research, and to the investigation of natural phenomena, much of which he embodied in his multi-volume work entitled *Kitāb al-Ḥayawān* (The Book of Animals). This work contains the results of his researches into the world of nature as a whole, and while some of it is of doubtful scientific value, there runs through it all a strong belief that the sciences not only have progressed from past to present but that they will continue to progress indefinitely into the future. This theory of scientific progress was echoed by many practicing scientists, who often set forth their faith in it in the introductions to their scientific works. The geometricians, astronomers, and physicians were particularly insistent that their own contributions constituted an advance upon the works of the ancients.

Such optimism, however, was not shared by all Muslim thinkers. Some believed that certain sciences were subject to decrease and increase. Others, who bewailed the state of morality and knowledge in their times, were inclined to maintain that the universe was constantly "running down," and that the sciences, like other branches of knowledge, would eventually suffer the same fate. Even philosophers like Fārābī tended to see in their philosophical system a consummate and perfect whole, leaving little if any room for intellectual advancement for later generations. Such philosophical conservatism, coupled with the even more prevalent conservatism of religious scholars, who believed that all virtue and knowledge had found their perfection in the Prophet and his generation, acted in time to dampen scientific enthusiasm. This conservatism, coupled with the fact that the Muslim world had broken up into various power blocs with the advent and establishment of military feudal regimes, curtailed the freedom of intercourse among Muslim scientists and confined their horizons in the later periods. Individual scientists of renown could still produce original work, but the attitude to knowledge as a collective pursuit, which characterized their activity in the classical period, was no longer in evidence.

Geography

A keen curiosity about the site of events characterized Muslim learning from its earliest days. This curiosity derived from the attempt made by religious scholarship to locate and identify the placenames in the Koran, *Ḥadīth*, and pre-Islamic poetry. A clear religious significance was attached to the proper identification of stations of pilgrimage, tombs of companions of the Prophet and holy men, and various places associated with the life and conquests of the Prophet and the first four caliphs. This religious curiosity was soon coupled with trade and with the need to map out trade routes. Finally, the early Arab Muslim rulers were interested in learning as much as they could about the regions they had conquered, and the institution of the postal system as well as the maintenance of roads and bridges were important means to achieve administrative centralization. These three impulses, the religious, the commercial, and the administrative, combined to produce Islamic geography.

From its earliest days, therefore, Islamic geography was a discipline that spanned many sciences, dealing with subjects that we would not now associate with geography and catering to a wide variety of social interests. A broad gamut of sciences, from astronomy to grammar, was pressed into its service while a broad range of documentation from state archives to mariners' tales was used to amplify its descriptions of the earth and of its various regions. As foreign cultures began to take firmer hold within Islam, and Greek philosophy and science permeated intellectual life, a vision of the world began to emerge based on Indian astronomy, Persian ideas about the regions of the earth, and, most important of all, Greek geographical ideas, especially those of Ptolemy. The work of Ptolemy was to exercise the same influence on Islamic geography that Aristotle and Plato had done on Islamic philosophy.

This Ptolemaic universe was believed by ninth- and tenth-century geographers to have the earth as its center. The earth rests in the midst of nine concentric spheres, seven of which have one planet each. The four elements that make up the first seven spheres are arranged in ascending order as earth, water, air, and fire, and each is present in the other potentially. The mineral, plant, and animal life that makes up the sublunary region is connected with the higher regions of this order. This universe of elements and spheres exercises a marked influence on man by shaping and determining his geographical environment. The order of the universe is a sign of God's creative wisdom.

The earth itself, according to some geographers, is in a state of ebb and flow, of lands becoming seas and seas receding to form lands. This, according to some scientists and geographers, is not an eternal movement, as Indian astronomers believed. Through it all can be detected a constant decrease in the physical matter of the universe, a nature that is being slowly depleted of its power. Muslim cosmologists and geographers saw in this a proof of the fact that the world would eventually come to an end, a confirmation of the religious view of a universe that began in physical perfection and would one day end in physical collapse.

Following the Persian idea of latitude, Muslim geographers of the classical period divided the earth into seven latitudinal regions, all of which lie north of the equator. The regions lying to the extreme north are far from the sun and therefore cold and snowbound. The regions lying to the extreme south, near the equator, are adversely affected by the sun and heat. The earth itself was believed to be spherical in shape and to be surrounded on all sides by the encircling ocean. An image frequently employed by contemporary geographers was that of a grape floating in water. The temperature of the air, the change of seasons, the elevation of the land, the movement of the winds were all factors that affected psychological temperament, physical characteristics, moral virtues, and the reason of man. Muslim geographers generally believed that the fourth or median region was the most temperate of all because a moderate climate produces the most perfect bodies as well as the most perfect minds. Iraq was often said to be the center of this region and was therefore the home of ancient civilizations. Geographical factors, therefore, are chiefly responsible for determining man's physical as well as cultural attributes. The arts and sciences of ancient nations could not have arisen if these nations had not inhabited temperate regions. One can therefore speak of classical Muslim geography as being, in general, deterministic. Certain regions were known to breed unchangeable qualities of character like generosity or miserliness, sternness or frivolity, aggressiveness or pacifism. Prophecy itself was said to have appeared only within the fourth region, the implication being that even divine intervention in human affairs had to conform to the geographical order of the universe.

Muslim geographers of the classical period were in their great majority city men. However, the unit of their geographical imagination was not the city but the region. The basis of society was quite clearly agrarian, and, although cities were described as being essential to human civilization, they were frequently pictured as unhealthy and quick to fall to ruin. The geographers often recorded the agricultural produce of each region as well as their taxation figures in various periods. Accordingly, their works contain a wealth of economic information, of interest to the state administrator as well as to the itinerant merchant. The fact that diverse regions were noted for the production of diverse agricultural produce was taken to be a sign of the balance that God had instituted in the world, making these regions interdependent and thus stimulating trade among them.

But geographers were also alive to the demand of their readers for entertainment in the style of *Adab*. Therefore, they frequently include in their accounts the "marvels" of various regions and cities, and defended the inclusion of these marvels either by claiming that God could indeed create whatever He willed or by stating that their purpose was to entertain and amuse their audience. In any case, the world of the supernatural, of demons and jinns and hybrid creatures of various sorts, was never absent from the works of even the most sceptical geographers. The world, after all, was a marvelous creation, and reversals of natural custom were an ordinary, indeed providential, part of the scheme of the universe. Wherever he turned, man was enveloped by nature and the cosmos. Body, character, and mind were products of man's natural environment, and geographers would illustrate this fact by reference to all the sciences that could explain this intimate relationship.

Chapter Nine

THE GOVERNANCE OF THE *UMMA*

Political Thought

Islamic political thought in the classical period may, broadly speaking, be divided into three major streams that had little or no connection with one another. The first may be termed the philosophical stream and may be defined as the attempt on the part of certain Muslim philosophers to recast the political philosophy of Plato into an Islamic mould. The second stream in Islamic political thought is the one that grew out of *Adab*, or belles-lettres, and may be defined as the attempt on the part of certain Muslim thinkers to recast the political wisdom-literature of Greece, Persia, India, and their own historical experiences into an Islamic mould. The third stream and by far the largest in volume, though not necessarily in influence, is the one which grew out of jurisprudence *(fiqh)* and may be defined as the attempt on the part of certain Muslim jurists to define the nature of the Caliphate or the Sultanate, either in theoretical or in practical terms. I shall deal with each stream separately and in the order outlined above.

Philosphical political theory in Islam is rightly associated with the philospher Fārābī. It was he above all others who attempted to demonstrate how Platonic political thought could be relevant to a society ruled by revealed law. For Fārābī, this was not an exercise in academic speculation but an ambitious program of political reform that aimed at restructuring the political foundations of a religious society. Fārābī was even less successful than Plato had been in creating a new type of commonwealth, but his ideas were to exercise a lasting fascination despite the fact that their direct influence on later political movements was probably negligible.

In constructing his political theory, Fārābī faced at least three major obstacles. The first was that Greek political philosophy was bounded by the geographical as well as cultural horizons of the *polis,* the classical Greek city state, whereas the horizons of Islam were limited only by the presence of the *umma*, a socioreligious rather than a geographical unit. The second obstacle was the Platonic philosopher-king, the prime mover of Platonic government, a sort of legislator-ruler-priest. The equivalent in Islam could only be the Prophet, for it was he who had set down for all time the ethical and political precepts of the Islamic *umma*. The third obstacle was the question of revelation. The Muslims possessed the very words of God. They were, in a real sense, *His umma*, and he was their ruler. No earthly commonwealth such as Plato had attempted to describe could possibly claim the ultimate allegiance of Muslims, irrespective of its inherent rationality. These three obstacles, the *polis*, the philosopher-king, and the law are the dominant themes in Fārābī's political writings. From them, he had to weave an intricate web of political thought and political relationships, a task that was, in a sense, more difficult and fraught with greater danger than the task of Plato himself.

In Fārābī's world view, the political realm encompasses nations as well as cities. Politics is both a theoretical and a practical activity. Its theoretical part embodies truths that are self-evident to all nations at all times. Its practical part means the ability to translate that theory into rules and norms relevant to particular nations and particular cities. This view of politics suggests the existence of universal norms and rules of conduct, and is, in itself, a step that goes beyond the classical Greek political notion of a world divided between Greek city states on the one hand and *barbaroi* on the other. Among such universal political rules or norms is the rule that human association is necessary for the perfection of individual virtue. Man can only attain that perfection in the company of other men. Ethics finds its perfection in politics: the unit finds its perfection in the whole. The whole for Fārābī is constituted by "nations and cities." The smallest unit of organization is the household. The harmony of the sociopolitical macrocosm is reflected in the harmony of the microcosm, and vice-versa.

If politics is the art or skill that translates theory into practice, it must provide for the establishment of a human community through a process of education that encompasses both the principles and the means to put them into practice. This process of education must take account of the diverse natures and abilities of men as well as their diverse historical experiences. It is not enough for this process to establish the theoretical principles of ethics and politics. It must also lead mankind to accept these principles, if not by rational demonstration then by rhetorical, literary, or allegorical means. In other words, an individual life of virtue, which finds its perfection in a community of virtuous people, requires an education either in philosophical truths or in similes and images of that truth. But since, for Fārābī, the majority of mankind can comprehend the truth only through images rather than through theory, and since politics aims at the perfection of mankind in its totality, it follows that the philosopher-king of classical Greek political theory also needs to be a prophet, i.e., an expounder of philosophy in popular terms, a philosopher of the masses. For it is only in the mass that mankind can attain ultimate perfection. Therefore, political philosophy must be complemented by religion if it is to reach and educate the masses and to transform their lives in the direction of perfect virtue. Religion, so to speak, is the reflection of philosophy in the souls of the multitude, and the perfect philosopher is the one who combines in his person philosophical knowledge, practical skill in legislating for a particular community, and the power to persuade or coerce the community to accept his point of view.

Accordingly, we arrive at a notion of politics that transcends the boundaries of the Greek *polis* to include a sort of utilitarian concept of the greatest good for the greatest number. The philosopher-king becomes, for Fārābī, a legislator, a prince, a supreme ruler, an *imām*. The Law is not only retained, but its status is enhanced by being made to reflect, at its best, the philosophical principles that furnish it with its theoretical foundations.

The second stream in Islamic political thought is far more diffuse and far less amenable to systematic analysis. This is the stream that I have described as stemming from *Adab* or belles-lettres, where the attempt is made to tap the political wisdom of the ancients, especially Persia, for the service of Muslim rulers. I shall, therefore, describe its characteristics in general and attempt to relate the activities of its practitioners to social and political developments in Islamic history. The term "mirror of princes" literature is sometimes applied to this body of political thought, and this is a convenient starting point for a discussion of its general outlines.

Early Muslim rulers were fond of history and romance, and the class of courtiers that soon surrounded the early caliphs satisfied the curiosity of their masters by writing works on the history of the Arabs and of other nations as well as on poetry, tribal romance, and ancient wisdom. As the Muslim state began to establish its basic institutions, the empire that made the greatest impact on Muslim imagination was the Persian. The view became current in the eighth century that the Muslims were the heirs of the Persians in government, and this view was further reinforced when the Muslim empire itself shifted its center of gravity eastward. Persian history was, of all ancient histories, the one most familiar to Muslim men of letters in the classical period. The successive kings and dynasties, the various religions of ancient Persia, and "Persian wisdom" were familiar subjects in the curriculum of the Muslim *adīb*, or man of letters.

The Persians were thought to have excelled in the art of government. The greatness of their empire was reflected in a body of political wisdom and, at its height, that empire was thought to have enjoyed great material prosperity, order in its administration, and the allegiance of many nations. Historians and men of letters strove to give an account of the political wisdom that infused Persian statecraft. Thus, the Persians were said to have been the first to recognize the alliance between kingship and religion that was responsible for justice. Justice, in turn, produced prosperity, stability, and order. The building of cities, equitable taxation, and the maintenance of canals, roads, and frontier posts were the expressions of political statesmanship. Some Muslim thinkers detected a relationship between Persian political wisdom and Greek political philosophy. Thus, certain Persian monarchs were said to have been disciples of Plato and were themselves philosopher-kings.

This idealization of Persian statecraft by many Muslim *adībs* led to the emergence of a new type of political writing, the political manual intended for rulers or men of power. These manuals of politics are often reminiscent of the method, if not the philosophy, of Machiavelli. First comes the general rule and this is then followed by historical examples proving its validity in particular instances. Since these manuals were often addressed to men of authority by men of scholarship, they betray the expectations of the latter for a political role at the highest level of government. Thus, in emphasizing the alliance between kingship and religion, many of these manuals are directly advocating an alliance between government and the class of religious scholars. In many of these books of government the villains are the feudal landlords, who, if allowed too much freedom, are apt to decentralize government and to fragment authority. Accordingly, in addition to their emphasis on the justice of the ruler, these manuals also emphasize the importance of centralization in preserving dynastic unity. The ruler should at all times keep in touch with the daily affairs of government and should only surrender his authority to men whose allegiance to him is total and secure.

Justice, the alliance between kingship and religion, centralization—these are major themes in this genre of Islamic political thought. Upon these principles depend the prosperity and peace of Muslim government. Not surprisingly, the question of legitimacy is left out of such manuals. This question had, in the course of time, become academic and was debated by jurists rather than the scholar-courtiers who were more intimately concerned with the dynamics of government. In any case, the question of legitimacy was frequently a "hot" one and too delicate to handle, especially in the early days of a dynasty. Rather, we find in these manuals a pragmatic acceptance of the ruler, as if the very fact of rulership was itself a sign of divine favor. This is especially true of manuals written in the days when the authority of the Abbasid caliphate had shrunk and when political power in Islam was assumed by a succession of Persian, Turkish, and Mongol dynasties, most of whom adopted the new name "sultan," thus appropriating for themselves temporal authority and leaving the caliph as a mere spiritual figurehead.

The new dynasties of the tenth and eleventh centuries were often feudal and military in structure and spirit. Accordingly, these political manuals devote a great deal of space to a discussion of the relationship between the ruler and his army, emphasizing such questions as the prompt payment of troops, training exercises, and military strategy. However, the scholars who wrote these manuals projected their own ideals of learning onto the image of the ruler, who is repeatedly advised to consort with men of scholarship rather than with drinking companions, who serve only to corrupt him and to tarnish his public image. This image must be carefully cultivated by the ruler, who is urged to be merciful and just, in conformity with the view that he is God's shadow on earth. Like God, the ruler must know the "secrets of men's hearts," and to this end he must employ a large army of spies who would report to him on the affairs of his kingdom and alert him to the possibility of rebellion. His attention to matters of state should not be diverted by amusements or by the influence of royal women, drinking bouts, excessive hunting, and so forth. In none of these manuals do the people, *en masse*, play an active role in state government. From them, the ruler demands obedience. To them, he must be an object of fear. He should frequently impress them with his might. Royal qualities like justice, generosity, and clemency serve only to emphasize the distance to be kept between ruler and subjects, for when he raises some to be members of his retinue, this is to be interpreted as a mark of exceptional royal favor. The ruler, in short, is a sort of god-scholar, and the majesty of his office resides essentially in the twin attributes of power and knowledge, the two traditional divine attributes of Islamic theology.

I arrive, finally, at the third stream of Islamic political thought, the stream that grew out of *fiqh*. What we are concerned with here is legal as opposed to philosophical or *adabī* political thought. In fact, the majority of medieval Muslim thinkers believed that political thought was a branch of jurisprudence and treated it in a legalistic spirit. This tradition of political thought parallels in many important ways the evolution in the social standing and the political role of the scholarly class in Islamic history. Looked at from this angle, we find that early political thought (up to and including the systematic recording of the *Ḥadīth* in the ninth century) is in a real sense utopian, backward-looking, idealistic. This tallies with the historical fact that in this early period of Islamic history, the scholars as a *class* had not yet arrived at a satisfactory accommodation with the state. Their reflections on the caliphate and on power in general are characterized by a powerful longing for the "golden age" of the first four caliphs, a period they considered normative for all later Islamic history. This is quite evident if we examine the corpus of the *Ḥadīth*, which acquired definite form in the ninth-century and much of which actually represented the ninth-century sentiments and opinions of the scholars who selected, collected, and sometimes forged these reports.

A hundred years later, this picture was to change in a dramatic fashion. With the rise of Persian and Turkish military-type dynasties in the Muslim world, the spiritual and temporal authority of the caliphate was in eclipse. The *ʿulamāʾ* class, who had looked to the caliphate to provide spiritual continuity, if not leadership, were now left leaderless. Slowly but surely, the *ʿulamāʾ* began to reflect in their writings an image of their own increasing importance as the guarantors and guardians of *Sharīʾa*, a role hitherto assumed by the caliphate. Increasingly it is seen in their political theory that it is their own preservation that is paramount in their minds rather than the preservation of the caliphate. They have become the elect of God. They are, as one ancient Muslim scholar put it, "the witnesses of God on earth." They immortalize their own kind in biographical dictionaries, which now (eleventh century onwards) proliferate throughout the Islamic world. This is also reflected in a change in their political role, for we find many of them actively involved in the political turmoil of the tenth, eleventh, and twelfth centuries, and there are several instances of judges ruling cities and regions as independent governors. With time, the qualifications of the caliphate become increasingly those of a scholar, less and less those of a saintly or pious individual. In other words, when they speak of the caliph, they mean a man of their own class rather than a paragon of virtue.

This, in brief, is the social and historical framework pertaining to the development of Islamic political theory of the juristic kind. It remains for us to examine in detail the views current in these two periods, i.e., the period up to the ninth century and the period that followed. Before we begin, let me briefly note some of the terms used by political theorists. In addition to the word "caliph," the theorists often used the term *imām*, a rather flexible term denoting a ruler. It could also mean a leader of prayers as well as a prominent scholar. In technical language, the term "great imamate" was a synonym for caliphate. (The term *imām*, however, had a totally different meaning for Shīʿites.) Every caliph is an *imām* but not every *imām* is a caliph.

As we have already seen, the early history of the caliphate is influenced by the role of the scholars as well as by the history of political leadership in Islam. Thus, when Abū Bakr became the first caliph, many voices, as noted above, were heard disputing his election. His claim was defended later on and Sunnī Islam always upheld his caliphate as legitimate. The next two caliphs were also generally recognized as legitimate. The first serious problem arose with ʿAlī, whose legitimacy was never universally recognized. When the Umayyads finally came to power, they regarded themselves as successors to the first three caliphs. ʿAlī, it was argued, was not a caliph. This position, however, was disputed in many pious circles, and the Medina Law School was especially important in its religious and political opposition to the Umayyads. The Medinese were not as enthusiastic about the Umayyads as they had been about the early caliphs.

When the Umayyads were in turn overthrown by the Abbasids, the problem of the caliphate became, once again, crucial. The Abbasids were originally a revolutionary Shīᶜite movement whose rejection of the Umayyads was total. Soon, however, the Abbasids shed their revolutionary origins, came to rely increasingly on Sunnite sentiments, and asserted their special right to the caliphate as cousins of the Prophet. They recognized ᶜAlī rather than the Umayyad Muᶜāwiya* as the legitimate caliph, and Abbasid historians as well as propagandists often referred to the period of Umayyad rule as a period of *mulk*, or kingship, rather than a caliphate. *Mulk* in pious Muslim circles of the period carried exactly the same connotation as the word *rex* had in the Roman Republic: it signified arbitrary and willful government. In any case, the whole question of ᶜAlī's caliphate was reopened in Islam. The problem was by no means an academic one; rather, it deeply divided the Muslim community on the question of legitimacy and political allegiance.

The *Ḥadīth* was recorded and systematized in this period. In their majority, political *Ḥadīths* deal with the question of obedience to just and unjust rulers. The overriding view is that a caliph or ruler must be obeyed, even if he rules unjustly. He may be advised, but he cannot be overthrown. A number of *Ḥadīths* refer to a more ideal period when there was a "genuine" caliphate, and some restrict the number of caliphs to two, three, or four. One recurrent *Ḥadīth* states that there will be twelve caliphs and then anarchy. The emphasis here falls on the early glory of Islam, which will last for twelve caliphates. These conflicting *Ḥadīths* were, of course, a reflection of the conflicts of the early schools of Sunnī law and of their varying interpretations of the legitimacy of power. Thus, the early Ḥanbalite lawyers at first recognized only three caliphs and only later accepted ᶜAlī. Throughout the classical period, Ḥanbalism maintained an idealistic view of the legitimacy of power. Other schools of law were more "liberal" in their views, but none of them succeeded in reconciling their theories with what was actually happening in their own days, i.e., in the ninth century.

Gradually, opinion seemed to crystallize around the view now backed by *Ḥadīth*, that there were four rightly-guided caliphs: that the caliphate lasted only 30 years and was then followed by *mulk*.

This was a compromise to which both Sunnites and some Shīᶜites could subscribe. The caliphate hence was regarded as an ideal and temporary institution, restricted to four most excellent men. The Ḥanbalite view was the one that dominated this early stage of political thought. In their view, only the early period was doctrinally and politically important. The later period, if it is discussed at all, is discussed only in so far as obedience to the ruler is emphasized. These early views were meant to unify Muslim public opinion and also to combat heresy, which frequently arose from conflicts in political loyalties.

The most complete definition of this early Ḥanbalite political theory is found in the work of Abū Yaᶜlā* (d. 1065). He argued that the Imamate is necessitated by law, not reason, since reason as such does not impose any legal obligations. The caliph must be from Quraysh, must be just and learned, free and mature, and be the best man in religious and scholarly terms. He can be elected either by the unanimous decision of "men who bind and loosen" (an extremely ancient Near Eastern idea denoting men of influence in the community and found as early as the *Epic of Gilgamesh*) or he can win his post by victory, provided he fulfills the other qualifications. Only anti-Sharīᶜa laws are to be disobeyed. Otherwise, even an unjust *imām* is to be tolerated. The views of Abū Yaᶜlā still retain a difference between the first four caliphs and the rest, even though these latter were loosely referred to as *imāms* and caliphs. The emphasis throughout is on obedience.

This was roughly the position reached when Māwardī* (d. 1058) appeared on the scene. Māwardī's work has been more extensively studied than that of any other thinker on the theory of government in Islam, and his work profoundly influenced later writers of Islamic political thought. Māwardī begins by listing the qualifications of the caliph: Quraysh ancestry, piety, knowledge and ability to protect Islam. But his most important contribution to the debate on the caliphate was to regard the caliphate of the contemporary Abbasids as a caliphate in the full sense. The earlier view that the true caliphate had ended with the first four is now abandoned and only one caliphate has lasted: that from the death of the Prophet right down to contemporary caliphs, including both Umayyads and Abbasids. This vigorous defense of the caliphate may well have been inspired by Māwardī's desire to defend the caliphs of his own day from the increasing encroachment of Buyid* princes with Shīᶜite leanings. Again, the early theory had presumed that only the best *(al-afḍal)* could be a caliph. This was true only of the first four. Later caliphs were either ignored or not treated on the same level. Māwardī was to argue that the consensus of Muslims legitimized later caliphs, and while the first four may have been the ideal precedent, the caliphate as an institution was enshrined in a continuous line. If the best was not available, then whoever was best able to cope with current political necessities may be chosen for the office. This legitimization of the caliphate by consensus, generally understood by Māwardī to mean a consensus of Muslim scholars, represents an increased awareness by these scholars of their own importance in determining the norms of political life. The community, i.e., the community of scholars, now steps forward to put its seal of approval upon the caliphate. Unlike the Ḥanbalites, who accepted any *imām*, however unjust, Māwardī argued that a caliph can lose his office if he is not morally upright. So, all in all, while Māwardī legitimizes the caliphate of his day, he rejects the theoretical quietism of the Ḥanbalites, and, here too, one may detect the growing selfconfidence of the scholars of his generation.

The next great writer on political theory is the famous Ghazālī. His work, like Māwardī's, defends the legitimacy of the contemporary Abbasid caliphs. Ghazālī was also in favor of the political order introduced into Islam by the Seljuq empire,* best represented in the work of its famous vizier, Niẓām al-Mulk,* whom Ghazālī greatly admired. Ghazālī argued that the caliphate is a permanent necessity. Only when a caliph is present is the whole judicial framework of Islam legitimate. The caliphate cannot possibly lapse or be interrupted, for then the Muslims would be living in sin. (This is probably an echo of the Shīᶜite doctrine of the Imāmate.) Accordingly, the requirements for the caliphate are lowered to make room for almost any candidate. Political necessity may dictate that an unjust caliph may be elected. The only prerequisite is the Quraysh ancestry, since *Ḥadīths* to this effect are incontestable. Otherwise, Ghazālī's caliph retains only a shadow of his former stature. Thus, in early theory, the caliph must lead his armies to battle. Ghazālī changes this requirement so that the caliph need only possess the support of the military groups of his day and age. The Turks often disregarded the orders of the caliph, but it is sufficient if they all pay lip service to him. Thus, the old functions of the caliphate can now be divided among various groups. The military function can be performed by the Turks or other similar groups. The function of chief judge, which belonged to the caliph in early theory, is given by Ghazālī to legal scholars. Again, in early theory, the caliph must be able to deal with political problems. In Ghazālī's view, however, it is enough to rely on good advisors, like Niẓām al-Mulk.

Ghazālī's caliph, therefore, is a spiritual symbol rather than a power. The necessity of preserving order and preventing anarchy is paramount in his thought, and in this his views tally with the views of Niẓām al-Mulk. Even the investiture of the caliph becomes, for Ghazālī, a question of the balance of power. If a man of power invests a caliph with his authority and this is generally accepted, then the appointment is valid because general acceptance is a form of consensus as well as a sign of divine favor. Here, too, the views of Ghazālī are reminiscent of the ideas of the famous Persian statesman. For example, Ghazālī refers to the caliph as the "Caliph of God," a term hitherto considered objectionable since earlier theory referred to him as "Caliph (or deputy) of the Prophet of God."

Ghazālī turns the Caliph into a representative figurehead of the Muslim community and a symbol of their unity, whose presence is absolutely necessary for the validity of legal judgments and of Muslim life in general. Older questions relating to his function and his qualifications (i.e., whether to elect the best or the second best, and so on) are shelved. The aim is no longer to define an ideal caliphate but to refashion an existing caliphate in spiritual terms and to accommodate it to the new power strucutre of the Seljuq empire. Ghazālī writes:

> An *imām* needs military assistance in order to demonstrate his power. . . and to enable him, when his supporters and troops are united, to suppress rebellions and fight unbelievers. . . . This is what we mean by assistance, and such assistance is currently available to that holy office *(al-jiha al-muqaddasa)*. For, of all mankind, power in our present age belongs to the Turks. God has exalted them for being the *imām's* loyal followers so that they have drawn closer to God by supporting the *imām* and subduing the enemies of his state. Belief in his caliphate, imāmate, and in the necessity to obey is an article of faith for them. . . . No other *imām* has ever enjoyed such support.

By the eleventh century, this new power structure had also produced another political office: the sultanate. The word "sultan" denoted power in a secular sense and was free of the religious associations of the word "caliph." It was now to gain currency among the various Turkish, Kurdish, and Mongol dynasties, none of whose rulers could of course aspire to the office of the caliphate because of the absolute prerequisite of Arab-Quraysh descent. The term was now to crop up increasingly in Islamic political thought. The destruction of Baghdad by the Mongols in 1258 and the murder of the last Abbasid caliph and his family was not as catastrophic an event as it has often been depicted, since the caliphate by that time had been reduced to quite a weak state. An alleged relative of this last caliph was produced by the Mamluk empire* of Egypt and Syria and installed as caliph in Cairo, but this Cairo caliphate was even less visible than the last Baghdad caliphs had been. Political theorists thus turned their attention to the problem of the political efficacy of the regime they served. Their works became less theoretical and more pragmatic, assuming the character of constitutional handbooks. Of this later tradition, only the works of two jurists will be discussed: Ibn Jamāʿa* and Ibn Taymiyya.* These two were contemporaries. Both lived during the period of greatest Mamluk expansion (mid-thirteenth to mid-fourteenth centuries) and both addressed themselves directly to the questions of contemporary government. In both we find a mixing of the two offices of caliph and sultan and a recognition of the preponderant importance of the latter.

Ibn Jamāʿa (d. 1333) followed the tradition of Ghazālī. But, while he justified the necessity of the caliphate by using traditional sources like the Koran and *Ḥadīth*, he turned around at once and justified the existence of the sultanate by use of the same sources. Thereafter, the focus of his attention is on the sultan, who is needed for the good of the people. It is now the sultan who is the shadow of God on earth, and obedience to him is comparable to obedience to God. The caliph delegates his powers to the sultan and thereafter one expects similar qualifications from both offices. Both are owed obedience, advice, and support. Both are expected to defend the *Sharīʿa*, carry out legal punishments, appoint judges, and collect taxes. The two offices merge into one by the fiction of delegation, theoretical continuity is maintained with the past, and the sultan now occupies a secure place in Islamic political theory.

Ibn Taymiyya (d. 1328) is renowned both as a lawyer and as a theologian. He was a Ḥanbalite and his views reflect certain fundamental elements of the early Ḥanbalite theory of power. To Ibn Taymiyya, the consensus of the men in power is essential in establishing rulership. Thus, a sultan comes to power by subjugation or by public homage. In either case, he must be obeyed provided he is obedient to God. An unjust ruler is better than none, this being an echo of earlier Ḥanbalite theory, and rebellion is not permissible. His mixing up of caliph and sultan is also characteristic of this period, since his concern is not with legitimacy but with the establishment of communal order and peace. Only the *Sharīʿa* ultimately unifies the Muslims, and if a ruler, any ruler, carries out this law, he is to be regarded as just. If a ruler does not do so, this is his private concern, but obedience is in any case obligatory. This view is typical of the sentiments of the *ʿulamāʾ* during the period of Mamluk history when it was customary for them to support whomever was in authority until he was overthrown. The caliphate is now totally overshadowed by the far more important problem of preserving unity of the community; this now becomes the concern of scholars.

We have already seen that if the history of Islamic political theory is analyzed from the viewpoint of its theorists, the *ʿulamāʾ*, we can detect the increasing involvement of the scholar class in political affairs as well as the enhancement of their own self-image to the point where it is they rather than the caliphate who are the true guardians of the Muslim polity. Looked at thematically, the dominant theme was: Should we elect the best or should we be satisfied with the second best? This early theme finds its answer in Māwardī. The dominant later theme is: Should we have a caliph at all, and if so what is his relationship to the Muslim community in general and to the *ʿulamaʾ* in particular? These were the broad themes of Islamic political thought until the caliphate itself was abolished in 1924.

Chapter Ten

IBN KHALDŪN— THE GREAT SYNTHESIS

"MAN IS the product, not of his ancestry but of his social customs." This phrase, which Ibn Khaldūn uses more than once, is, I think, an appropriate starting point for this brief survey of his thought. If we examine the table of contents of the four volumes of the standard edition of his *Muqaddima* or *Introduction to History*, we find that the *Muqaddima* is divided, broadly speaking, into three major parts:

1) An account of historiography; its basic principles together with illustrations of typical errors committed by Arab Islamic historians.

2) An account of the science of human culture *(ilm al-ʿumrān al basharī)*; the principles of this science are for Ibn Khaldūn the basis of historical understanding. This science encompasses an account of basic social formations (e.g., nomadic, sedentary) and the rise of the state and of civilization together with the laws *(sunan)* that regulate their interaction. Copious historical incidents are cited as illustrations for these laws.

3) An account of Islamic institutions and sciences as they had evolved up to his own days in the fourteenth century.

In all this, there is a startling shift of emphasis. Medieval Islam had concerned itself primarily with man as an individual, with his soul, will, or reason, with the man-God relationship. For Ibn Khaldūn, however, questions about man are ultimately questions about society. This emphasis on society and civilization is the secret of Ibn Khaldūn's popularity in the nineteenth and twentieth centuries, the centuries that witnessed the rise of the social sciences: sociology, economics, and comparative culture. In the Arab world today, Ibn Khaldūn's *Muqaddima* enjoys greater esteem than ever before. For here, apparently, is a secular account of human civilization and of the laws that it obeys. This contemporary of Machiavelli, with whom he is often compared, is telling us that the final mover of history is not the mysterious ways of God but the laws of society and civilization; that it is not man's essence but rather man's existence that defines and controls his life.

* * *

We will now take up each part of the *Muqaddima* in turn and attempt to analyze its main conclusions. In the first part of the *Muqaddima*, devoted to historiography, Ibn Khaldūn makes a sweeping attack on the historians of his own and of previous generations. Most of their works are a mixture of myth and polemic. Because of their ignorance of the laws of social change, all of them, says Ibn Khaldūn, have failed in diagnosing the true causes of the rise and fall of dynasties and nations. They have been content to record the ups and downs of history without ever perceiving the deeper causes of events.

History, in reality, is information about association, which is in fact world culture, together with the various phases through which this culture passes by its very nature, such as wild and domestic existence, the social bond, and the modes of human domination. . .and the ensuing modes of government, states and their diverse ranks as well as the types of human labor. . . modes of acquisition and livelihood, the sciences and the crafts.

In appearance, history is an art which has to do with reporting the past. In reality, however, it is a science that analyzes the principles of social reality. The primary task of the historian, therefore, is to acquaint himself with the various modes that human culture assumes in order to distinguish truth from error in historical reports. Thus, the individual events of history passing before our eyes, the signs of human activity, both economic and intellectual, the changes brought about by revolutions and the turmoil of political life, the rise and fall of states, dynasties, or empires—in short, all the phenomena of social life around us are merely the symptoms of a deeper reality that controls them all. The science of culture provides the principles upon which the stories of history are built. Historical reports must be tested against these principles and, if found wanting, they must be rejected as either myth, polemic, or rhetoric. The particular event must always be understood against its social context; the individual is always subordinate to the universal; the single instance is always less significant than the general pattern. Historical truth is determined by context, and the context is the social stage at which the event occurs. The laws that determine social change furnish the historian with a tool that enables him to separate what could have happened from what could not. But these laws also mean that the world as seen by Ibn Khaldūn is rigid, orderly, perhaps even mechanistic. And this will become clearer when we discuss the second part of the *Muqaddima*, which deals with the science of human culture.

* * *

Islamic speculation about human society and civilization clearly antedated Ibn Khaldūn. Several prominent Arab historians before Ibn Khaldūn, as we saw above, had concerned themselves with deeper patterns of history. His work, therefore, stands within a certain philosophical tradition of historical writing that strove not merely to reproduce the past but to deduce or rationalize its significance. This is an aspect of his work that deserves to receive greater prominence, for it provides us with a more comprehensive understanding of the genesis of his science of culture. From earlier Muslim historians Ibn Khaldūn derived the attempt to discover the final structure of historical change. Some historians had tried to apply the exactitude of the natural sciences to history and thus concentrated their attention not on how the knowledge of an event was transmitted to them but rather on the event itself, its credibility or otherwise, and what truth and reality in history really meant.

From Muslim philosophy, Ibn Khaldūn derived his conception of science together with the methodology of the science that he self-consciously asserts to have invented, the science of culture. Muslim philosophy was for Ibn Khaldūn the most authoritative source of information in such fields as climate, geography, and psychology, all of which constitute the totality of the human environment within which social change takes place. His science of culture, then, continues two traditions: philosophical historiography and philosophy.

This, then, is the project of Ibn Khaldūn. History must be rescued and purified for political as well as religious reasons. Why political? Because when we purify history and remove all its myths, it can then serve as a guide to action, for history will then be found to be repetitive and to operate according to certain laws or rules. Why religious? Because the Koran also must be protected against all myths, fairy tales, and fabrications that have clung to it through the activity of bad exegetes.

The second step that Ibn Khaldūn takes, after rejecting *taʾrīkh* or historiography, is to move to an examination of events, which are the stuff of history. Ibn Khaldūn argued that an event, any event, can be explained from two points of view, the particular and the general. If we look at it from the particular point of view we ask: "*Did* it happen as reported?" If we look at it from a general point of view, we ask: "*Can* it happen?" Now, for Ibn Khaldūn, the general comes first: "*Can* it happen?" is more important than "*Did* it happen?" There is not much point in discussing whether X event took place if we know already that X is impossible.

How do we know whether X is possible or impossible? This is where Ibn Khaldūn takes his third step, the step of transforming the event into law, transforming history into lessons and rules. There are several ways of distinguishing between the possible and impossible. Events, according to Ibn Khaldūn, take place *in* nature; therefore they are, generally speaking, molded and shaped by natural conditions. A certain piece of land, for example, cannot support more than a certain population level. Another way of distinguishing and testing is that the cause of events, for Ibn Khaldūn, is proportionate to the size of events. The greater any event is, the more likely it is to have major causes. The rise and fall of dynasties, the rise and fall of arts and sciences, the rise and fall of great cities: all these are major events, and we cannot attribute them to single or minor causes. Once we understand the natural environment of history we are in a position to analyze it rationally, for nature has its laws and limits. And just as the general comes before the particular, so for Ibn Khaldūn man comes before the individual. Thus, when we study history our attention must be focused on human association, on the collective, on nations, tribes, dynasties, on large units, on human culture, or *ʿumrān*.

The heart of history then, the truth of history, its core, its inner reality, is found in human environment or culture. History makes sense only when we understand it as large units of human association rising, conquering, building, prospering, and then declining. Only then does history give way to the science of culture, *ʿilm al-ʿumrān*. Only then will history yield its lessons and morals, its laws and rules. Only then does history stop being the stories of this man or that battle, and become a science; and not only *a* science but *the* science, because it embodies and systematizes all the products of human culture.

As regards this new science, it would be natural for us to ask: to which family of sciences does it belong? Which science does it most closely resemble? For Ibn Khaldūn, this science belonged to the category of rational sciences. It was a science in the strictest sense of the term, possessing its own principles, methods, and conclusions. The knowledge derived from it is arrived at by demonstration *(burhān)*. It resembles rather closely the rational science of animal life *(ʿilm-al Ḥayawān)*. For Ibn Khaldūn, human societies are subject to a cycle of youth, maturity, and old age that is frequently compared by him to the biological life cycle of living organisms. Thus, states and societies also have their "natural ages" *(aʿmār ṭabīʿiyya)*. At each stage of development, societies exhibit certain characteristics that are relative to their "age," to where they are on what one may call the graph or chart of growth and development. To understand history means to understand the laws that govern each stage of social evolution; and just as the child behaves differently from an adult and an adult from an old man, so human societies behave differently according to their age. Accordingly, if one is pressed for a modern equivalent for Ibn Khaldūn's *ʿilm al-ʿumrān*, one might call it the science of social biology or, conceivably, the biology of civilization.

One way of analyzing the subject matter of this new science is, first of all, to list and analyze some of the more important terms and phrases that together constitute the dominant vocabulary of this science. I hope the following list has not overlooked any cardinal Ibn Khaldūnian concepts: primitive or nomadic society; state; social solidarity; tribal life; city life; power; religion; prophecy; necessities; luxuries; climate; custom; crafts; sciences; and economic livelihoods. The manner in which these interact in human history is the subject matter of the science of culture. But only a few of the more fundamental processes of interaction will be examined here.

For Ibn Khaldūn, human societies are, generally speaking, divided into two kinds. The first is Bedouin or nomadic society, the second is sedentary or urban. Each society has its own distinct social, political, economic, and psychological characteristics. One might almost consider them two different human environments, inhabited by two different types of human beings. Bedouin or nomadic society is called by Ibn Khaldūn primitive, tribal, and living on necessities. In this society, human life tends to be coarse and severe. People live close together in a tribal manner and are tied to each other by blood ties. There are few, if any, differences in wealth among them. In their attitude to life in general, they tend to be conservative and obey their tribal leader unquestioningly. They have no political institutions, no government in the true sense. What holds them together as a society is a social bond or tie, which Ibn Khaldūn calls *ʿaṣabiyya*, or social solidarity. *ʿAṣabiyya* enables primitive society to stay together as a human unit living in the harsh environment of the desert or wilderness. This mode of life endows Bedouin society with positive as well as negative attributes. On the positive side, Bedouins make excellent soldiers since their way of life renders them tough, disciplined, and loyal. They are, psychologically speaking, free and generous spirits who are quick to follow the call of a religion and to become its adamant adherents. On the negative side, they are frequently capable of vicious and wanton destruction, especially against cities, which are the unique achievements of sedentary civilization, but also against cultivators of land. One might perhaps compare Bedouin or primitive society to gangs of children roaming in a state of nature.

But just as children move into adulthood, so primitive society has a tendency to become sedentary or urban. There is an urge in all such societies to fulfill, actualize, or perfect themselves, to grow up. The laws and processes of nature are constantly attracting Bedouin society towards urbanization. This is one typical Ibn Khaldūnian law and, when examined with care, it turns out to be an application to social change of one of Aristotle's cardinal tenets, the change from potentiality into actuality. Primitive society is potentially urban society, just as the child is potentially the adult, the seed is potentially the tree, and so forth.

What is sedentary or civilized society? For Ibn Khaldūn, the basic form of this society is the city. There can be no civilized society, no civilization without a city. In a city, society is more complex than it is in primitive or Bedouin encampments. To begin with, city life is one of luxury, not of necessity. Furthermore, the politics of a city are more complex: a city has a ruler and a ruling dynasty, their deputies, army, tax departments, and bureaus of government. In short, there is a state *(dawla)*. From the economic point of view, the concentration of wealth breeds luxuries, among which Ibn Khaldūn includes the arts and sciences, that is, the intellectual aspects of the culture.

From the psychological point of view, a city man is quite different from a nomad. In a city the social bond, or *ʿaṣabiyya*, shrinks in strength by becoming confined to fellow citizens and then to family members, and thus ultimately grows weaker. So, in a city, man becomes more sophisticated, less conservative, more pacific, and ultimately weaker than other men with stronger or more congenital *ʿaṣabiyya*. Such factors as climate and diet also contribute to weakness. The history of a city is a history of the progressive unfolding of all these political, economic, climatic, and psychological tendencies, which grow critical as the state advances towards old age.

How does one society pass into the other? What stage does this process follow? For Ibn Khaldūn, the historical cycle always begins with primitive society and then proceeds to sedentary or civilized:

> We began with Bedouin culture because it is prior to all the rest. We have also begun by discussion of livelihoods because a livelihood is necessary and natural whereas the acquisition of learning is a luxury. . . and the natural is prior to the luxurious.

In primitive or Bedouin society as a whole, says Ibn Khaldūn, many tribal *ʿaṣabiyyas* are in operation at the same time. If we wish to maintain the parallelism with biology, we might compare them to the cells that seem to float in the slide of a microscope that is focused on a living organism. Each cell, or tribal unit, is in perpetual motion relative to the others, and is in a state of balance. From time to time, a change occurs. These cells coalesce to form more substantial units. The tribes that seem to circle each other merge to form new confederacies of tribes. There are two basic reasons for this according to Ibn Khaldūn. A leader, by the force and magnetism of his personality, mobilizes the tribes around a new inter-tribal *ʿaṣabiyya*, or else a religion arises that creates a new and transcendent *ʿaṣabiyya*. In either case, whether the *ʿaṣabiyya* is charismatic or religious, a nomadic or primitive society becomes mobilized and is ready for the transformation into a sedentary society. This mobilization can either lead to absorption by stronger societies or to the establishment of a new political society.

If this primitive society achieves victory, it enters the cycle of political growth. At first the ruling group of that society is still in possession of its primitive *ʿaṣabiyya*. Soon however, a life of necessities becomes a life of luxuries, the tribal chief becomes the city king, primitive economic exchange becomes commerce and industry, tribal hordes become regular army soldiers. It is then that the city-state reaches the height of its political, cultural, military, and economic power. This stage is followed by decline. The reasons for the decline are, for Ibn Khaldūn, social, political, and economic. As we have seen, long life in a city weakens the old bond of *ʿaṣabiyya*. The hardy nomad gives way to the effete citizen. The tribal ruler becomes the state dictator. The state itself extends its power over all aspects of life. Where the economy is concerned, this growth of centralization involves the increasing domination of the state over economic activity. The state becomes "the great market" *(al-sūq al-aʿẓam)*, at once the greatest consumer, supplier, and employer. Monopolistic practices by the ruler gradually begin to suffocate the free flow of business. To keep himself in power, the ruler needs a regular army to replace the disintegrated group that first upheld his dynasty. Therefore, he needs more money and more taxes imposed on an increasingly recalcitrant population. It is then that the state grows into old age and is ready for final collapse or fragmentation. According to Ibn Khaldūn, the entire cycle of a state, from beginning to end, takes normally three to four generations. This does not mean that every state necessarily dies after four generations, but only that, after four generations, calculated by Ibn Khaldūn as roughly a hundred and twenty years, a state is ready for collapse. This collapse, says Ibn Khaldūn, happens in either of two ways. The state is either attacked by a more primitive group with a stronger *ʿaṣabiyya* or else is fragmented from its peripheries by rebellious governors. Victory always belongs to the stronger of any two warring *ʿaṣabiyyas* and with victory a new state is ready to begin the cycle anew.

This, in brief, is the Ibn Khaldūnian cycle of social change. At each step, Ibn Khaldūn is quick to supply parallels with the world of living organisms. History becomes a storehouse of examples illustrating the various stages of rise, decline, and fall. The state moves from the strengths of youth to the "diseases" *(amrāḍ)* of old age. The secularism of Ibn Khaldūn's thought may best be observed in his attitude toward the role of religion and of God in history. For Ibn Khaldūn religion functions as a form of *ʿaṣabiyya* and hence religion is part of the growth cycle. For illustration, Ibn Khaldūn frequently quotes the prophetic *Ḥadīth*: "A prophet is sent only to a people who are already strong enough to protect him." In other words, the activity of God coincides with natural processes, and God, in the phrase of Ibn Khaldūn, "permits" *(ya ʾdhan)* certain states to decline and others to arise. Man is historically a creature of his social environment, not a creature of God.

* * *

The last part of Ibn Khaldūn's *Muqaddima*, which deals with the evolution of Islamic institutions and sciences, will be examined more briefly. This third part of the *Muqaddima* contains what is probably the most succinct account of the history of Islamic institutions and sciences to be found in any medieval writer. In it one still finds the best short histories of the Islamic sciences, education, political parties, and institutions, crafts, and other "intellectual" *(ʿilmī)* productions of Islamic civilization as these had developed up to his own days. These generally non-material aspects of culture are found to be extensions of the material. Knowledge is a reflection of a specific way of life, and human thought depends upon social evolution. The sciences for Ibn Khaldūn are ultimately crafts *(ṣināʿāt)*. They thrive, like other material crafts, only at the cultural stage in which luxury makes their appearance possible. States, likewise, engender the institutions that are appropriate to their particular stage of evolution. This relationship of dependence between society and its intellectual products raises the most perplexing question of this last part of the *Muqaddima*. What happens to the arts and sciences as one state falls and another arises? Does Ibn Khaldūn believe in the cumulative progress of knowledge or does he believe that knowledge has its ups and downs just like political society? Instances can be found throughout the *Muqaddima* to support both assertions, i.e., that knowledge grows cumulatively as well as the view that knowledge shares in the collapse of political societies. Many ancient sciences have been irredeemably destroyed, says Ibn Khaldūn. But many new sciences have also been added and one must naturally assume Ibn Khaldūn's agreement with this second view also, especially when one bears in mind the claim he had advanced above of having himself discovered a new science.

Whatever the final answer to this problem of progress in Ibn Khaldūn, it remains clear to me, at any rate, that Ibn Khaldūn believed that the cycle of history and social change is eternal, having neither a beginning nor an end. He has constructed a science of social change, the end of which is the correction of historical reports. One aspect of this new science, one end, is descriptive, to describe what really happens in history, to go beyond history into meta-history. Nevertheless, Ibn Khaldūn also believed that the new science would have a practical purpose, that it is not only descriptive but prescriptive, i.e., to prescribe to statesmen and rulers what needs to be done in order to preserve *ʿumrān*. The new science, therefore, is not solely an adjunct to history but also to political science. This is where Ibn Khaldūn believed that the preservation of *ʿumrān* coincides with the *Sharīʿa*, the Islamic law of life, whose ultimate objective is also the preservation of *ʿumrān*. For, in purifying history of its myths, one is also protecting the Koran and the whole edifice of religion from the fabrications that have clung to it through the activity of bad historians or credulous commentators. We arrive finally at the Ibn Khaldūnian synthesis, a new science of culture that aids and complements the *Sharīʿa*, making explicit what in the *Sharīʿa* is only implicit, describing and prescribing for social welfare by reason what the *Sharīʿa* prescribes by revelation. A natural philosophy of history is synthesized with a project for social and religious reform.

Chapter Eleven

PAST AND PRESENT IN CONTEMPORARY ARABIC THOUGHT

THIS CONCLUSION is written with two principal aims in mind. The first is a critical examination of certain contemporary Arab views on classical Arab Islamic culture while the second is an attempt to formulate my views on the problem of the past and the present, that is, what has become widely known in the Arab world today as the question of the *turāth*, or heritage. I will begin by arguing that the two issues, that is, the critical examination as well as the individual formulation of opinion, are intimately connected. I will further attempt to show that (1) scholarly "detachment" is a luxury we cannot afford in the Arab world today and that (2) the problem of the *turāth* is highly polemical, so much so, in fact, that in the interests of accuracy if of nothing else, it is incumbent upon me to address the reader from within this polemic rather than from outside it.

When I speak of "detachment," I am referring not to the objective scholarly standards commonly obtaining in the study of history, but rather to the "detachment" of the *persona* of the Arab scholar from his political environment. In other words, it is not possible for an Arab academic working in the field of classical Arab Islamic history and culture to avoid embroilment in polemics. Arab society is increasingly demanding that its academics, "the new *ʿulamāʾ*," not only write in Arabic but also that they justify the relevance of their research to their own society. When academics come forward to speak on the question of the *turāth*, they are given political labels by their Arab audience. Some are said to be liberal "Westernizers," others are Islamic "reactionaries"; some are "infantile Marxists," others are "nationalist apologists" of one sort or another; some are Hegelian "idealists," others are mere "imitators" of one leading Western luminary or another. One cannot dwell too long on the labels themselves, but one must be fully aware of the act of labelling. Let me add that this can often be stimulating because it forces one to seek to discover the relevance of whatever obscurity one happens to be working on to one's immediate surroundings. In Afro-Asian societies as a whole, history possesses greater political immediacy and relevance than it does in Europe and America.

Accordingly, when one examines the works of contemporary Arab writers on the question of *turāth*, one finds that they all share, at least, a polemical style. There is an urgency about this style, a sense of impending doom but also a sense of promise. One often finds in these writers the image of a man standing at the crossroads: one path leads to progress and prosperity, the other to political calamity, eternal damnation. A new society is beckoning if only we can reach out and grab the rope dangling before us. A multitude of opinions is frequently reduced to a couple of alternatives. It is Marxism or the abyss. It is Islamic fundamentalism or Satan. It is technology and rationalism or ruin. A deafening cacophony from which one often longs to escape but cannot. Eventually one learns to live with it and even to benefit from it.

I am now going to sketch briefly the historical background of this debate on the question of the heritage, using the broadest possible brushstrokes. It would seem to me that the Arab intellectual scene of the twenties and thirties was more closely knit than it is today. The intellectual giant of the period, Ṭāha Ḥusain, would write a book, and the echoes would soon be heard all over the Arab world, through the medium of two or three literary magazines that everyone who was anyone in the intellectual field would read. The debates were conducted on an epic scale. Nowadays, however, the pendulum seems to have swung to the other side. Writers do not stir up as much controversy as they used to. Is this a reflection of increasing Arab political fragmentation? (I use the word "reflection" advisedly.) The answer is largely yes. The dream of Arab unity was shattered by the logic of the *raison d'état*. Universalism was dissolved to Erastianism.

When one reads these contemporary works, one discerns another theme that reinforces this fragmentation: the trauma of 1967. The crushing defeat of 1967 was felt most keenly perhaps by the intellectuals, who are now drawn increasingly from the ranks of journalists and new academics and thus from a much wider variety of social backgrounds. This magnetic attraction between journalism and academic life was highlighted by the trauma of 1967. The journalists served up the frightful news: the academics were practically implored to comment on them. And they were the more likely to respond because increasing numbers of these academics were drawn from the middle or lower classes, whose lives, hopes, and expectations had then reached a state that physicists call "critical mass." In other words, many more intellectuals were now involved and drawn from a much wider variety of social backgrounds. The clearly enunciated, measured tones, and gentlemanly polemics of the Arab salons of the twenties were now giving way to a sound resembling an orchestra tuning up.

The year 1967 was extremely important not only because it was felt to be so by most contemporary writers but because it catalyzed three basic concerns of Arab intellectuals. More accurately, perhaps, it helped to focus the on-going search for three super-tribes: the Islamic, the Arab/nationalist, and the Marxist. Thus, when the Syro-Egyptian union broke up in 1961, this was a defeat for the Arab nationalist super-tribe. The Islamic super-tribe was not shaken to the same degree. The Marxist super-tribe was not even on the scene yet. In 1967, however, the final act in the rape of Palestine shook up all three super-tribes simultaneously. The *turāth* for most intellectuals began to assume a present dimension and a dramatic relevance. The lines between the super-tribes became more clearly delineated in the ensuing soul-searching. The torment of the Arab intellectual after 1967 is captured most poignantly perhaps by Abdullah Laroui, who describes that intellectual as a sort of Hamlet figure, torn between the need to think and the need to act—with the need to think winning by a comfortable margin. Perhaps this tells us more about Laroui than about the Arab intellectual, but let us proceed.

As we go back to the orchestra tuning up, we discern that the dominant themes that these writers are handling may best be understood in the form of the following questions: Where do we stand in relation to our past and where do we go from here? As we advance into the world, what do we do about this "long caravan we are dragging behind us," as one writer put it? Is this caravan real or is it a figment of our imagination? The writers engaged in this debate have already begun to divide each other in accordance with the labelling game alluded to above. Therefore, I shall say something about how they classify each other with respect to the problem of the past, and then I shall, myself, enter the polemic and offer my own reflections, for whatever they are worth.

Laroui divides them into the Salafis (those who adopt the Islamic heritage as a viable, on-going tradition), the eclectics (those who pick and choose aspects of the heritage that they like), and the historicists, like himself, whose slogan may very well be: "Let us have our own Arab philosophy of history." Salafi, eclectic, historicist: this is a sharp classificatory insight. At its best, it is echoed by a writer like Nāṣīf Naṣṣār, who seems to be saying that what we need is another Ibn Khaldūn. At its worst, it is mutilated by a writer like al-Ṭayyib Tīzīnī, who runs wild trying to link up these three classifications (plus a few more of his own) with various social groups in earlier Arab history. Thus, Salafism is said to reflect a feudal outlook; eclecticism reflects the bourgeoisie attempting to make inroads into the feudal system, and so on. At its most dramatic, it is repeated by a writer like Mahdī ᶜĀmil, who argues that the fault is not in our heritage, but in our own bourgeois selves. (Incidentally, when I say that this classification is "echoed," I am not implying that all these writers necessarily copied Laroui, nor do I know for sure whether this classification is original with Laroui.)

Let me now enter this polemic myself by offering my own classification and asserting that, in our attitude to our past, *turāth* writers can broadly be classified as historically minded and non-historically minded. This, because it is a simplification, can only be a working hypothesis since some of us clearly are both. Let me begin with the non-historically minded. I call them so because some of us examine our cultural heritage much as if we were inhaling perfumes whose fragrance is forever sweet. These perfumes may be labelled "reason," "originality," or "freedom"; they may be identified as "mass revolution," "progressivism," or "proletariat consciousness," or they may be called "the cream of thought," "Islamic Pragmatism," or "progressive methodology." I call them non-historical because in each case these writers are resurrecting what they believe to be the *philosophia perennis* of Arab Islamic culture: certain attitudes, ideas, and states of mind that are selected from the totality of the cultural past and then identified as the keys that will unlock the doors of the future. This shopping around in the past is done on an extensive scale. We are urged to adopt not only certain aspects of the positive content of that heritage (e.g., the rationalism of the Muᶜtazilites, they being very popular now among many Arab liberal and leftist intellectuals), but sometimes we are more subtly urged to forget the content and adopt the methodology. The content, we are told, may be fleeting and time-bound, but the method "liveth forever." And when this desirable method is described, it frequently assumes the shape of poetic images like the "flame" of the past, its "authenticity," its "capacity for renewal." The best defense I can possibly offer for this viewpoint is the one that is implicit in the writings of many of these intellectuals, namely, if we do not shop around in our heritage, of what earthly use can it be to us? This, of course, is an important aspect of the problem of relevance that I gave some attention to at the beginning of these remarks.

My answer has been to maintain that by adopting a non-historical attitude to our *turāth*, we are, *a priori,* eliminating history as a dimension of understanding and substituting for it a series of desiderata that may or may not correspond to the actual needs and problems of Arab society. My second objection, which flows from the first, is that the non-historical shopping around assumes that contemporary Arab society is a monolithic whole whose needs, problems, and stages of evolution are all in some sense similar, an assumption that sociology, at least, teaches us to view with caution. My third objection is that the shopping baskets of the various shoppers contain a medley of metaphysical terms like "freedom," "revolutionary spirit," "rationalism," and so forth, which seem to mean quite different things to different writers, often depending upon these writers' real or presumed political commitments.

We now come to the historically-minded thinkers and to their attitude to the *turāth*. To begin with, many of them seem to be searching for an Arab philosophy of history. A great deal of contemporary discussion centers naturally on Ibn Khaldūn as a cultural counter-hero to Marx, perhaps, or as a thinker who formulated the great theory of development of Arab Islamic culture and history of the pre-Ottoman period. He is therefore commonly regarded as a thinker who is at least as useful as Marx as a philosophical tool for a historical understanding of the Arab past.

What does this search for an Arab philosophy of history involve? It involves, according to the historically-minded writers, "intellecting" our history in its totality in order to "possess," "overcome," "rediscover," or "transcend" it. (If any remain who still enjoy harmless Latin pedantry, one would summarize this attitude with the phrase *intelligo ut vincam*— I understand in order that I may overcome.) What does it mean to say of a given culture that one wants to understand it in order that one may overcome it? It means,

I think, that one understands as many of its aspects as possible in order that this may help one to advance in a desirable historical direction.

Chief among the models so far advanced by this group of thinkers for this kind of historical understanding of civilizations is a dialectic of one kind or another. This dialectic pits Arab Islamic civilization on the one hand *versus* Western civilization on the other. (The West, I believe, is the great cultural contender. Eastern civilization, e.g., Indian or Chinese, is simply not part of this cultural *gestalt*.) Arab Islamic culture must not "ape" the West but must stand opposite it, on an equal footing, in the classical pose of the thesis-antithesis confrontation. However, it can and must reflect it, not for invidious cultural comparisons but for fruitful cultural interaction. The dialectical synthesis that these history-minded writers are seeking is not always made explicit but often involves a view of a world civilization enriched with our own historical and cultural vividness.

I doubt whether the historically-minded writers would necessarily agree that this has been a fair summary of their views on the *turāth* at every point in the analysis. I myself find much in it that is fruitful. The search for a new civilizational synthesis, a new *muqaddima*, is a sign of health.

However, several qualifiers should, in my view, be added. In this brief study of classical Islamic culture, I have attempted to confine the discussion of that culture within its own historical horizons. The intellectual circuitry of that culture has been my main concern. To understand that circuitry, it has not seemed to me either necessary or desirable to discuss questions relating to the foreign origins or to the future of that civilization. Instead, I have tried to assemble and analyze its own independent classical "discourse."

The intimacy of the relationship between past and present, which is the source of the current debate on the *turāth*, is not of course a modern controversy. It has heated up at least once every century or so and seems to be reaching a boiling point in the last quarter of the present century. It is a recurrent crisis of Arab Islamic historical consciousness. In answer to the question what does one do with one's past one might be tempted to argue that the primary duty of the historian of ideas is to recognize it for what it is: a past. This past is not necessarily a storehouse of exportable maxims or truths, nor is it something to be understood in order to be "overcome," nor is it something to be analyzed in exclusive apposition to the West. Rather, I have tried to show how both culture *and* society functioned, or were articulated in their specific historical fields. In my view, the recognition of our distance from our *turāth* is at least as fruitful as our recognition of its intimate proximity. To say, as I said in my introduction, that classical Arab Islamic culture is locked into the life of modern Arabs and Muslims is to assert an evolutionary truism. But the Arab Islamic past is not necessarily the nearest thing there is to the Arab Islamic present, whatever *that* may be. There may indeed be social and economic resemblances to other contemporary societies that may be far more striking and influential than anything from the *turāth*. Men, says the Arabic proverb, resemble their own times more than they do their ancestors *(al-nās bi zamānihim ashbahu minhum bi ābā'ihim)*. And the late Marshall Hodgson wrote, "All modern societies have more in common with each other, especially on the decisive levels of historical action, than has any of them with its own pre-Modern antecedents." One may not wish to go this far, but whenever the question of the modern impact of the *turāth* is discussed such reminders of the overwhelming relevance of contemporaneity are always welcome.

It remains to add that I am not advocating antiquarianism where classical Arab Islamic culture is concerned, nor am I arguing that the problem of its modern relevance is insoluble. But I am inclined to believe that a certain detachment or even disengagement from that culture, a focusing instead on its specific historical networks would show that it is not so much the conclusions in the various classical disciplines that should interest us today but rather the accumulation of the diverse answers that earlier generations have given in diverse historical circumstances. This entails the investigation of the dominant preoccupations of each cultural generation in contrast or comparison with other generations, not in order to construct some hypothetical graph of progress, and certainly not to uncover the Platonic "form" of Islam, but rather to seek to understand the spectrum of cultural expression that Arab Islam has manifested and continues to manifest, and then, and only then, to try to pinpoint gaps. To take one example, the poverty of Arab Islamic theology in the last hundred years or so is one glaring gap on this cultural spectrum, and its absence is sorely felt whenever we nowadays encounter sweeping statements of the type "Islam believes that such and such" or "The Islamic view of this question is this and that." It is sorely felt also when we Muslims discuss issues like freedom, secularism, war, justice, and so forth, where theology is indispensable.

Therefore, there can be no alternative, in my opinion, to attempt accurately to determine the historical stages of the cultural evolution of Arab Islam. Furthermore, the equidistance of cultures from each other and from a supposedly ideal center is the moral of the story of cultures. While cultural "circuitries" do indeed resemble each other, there is little value to be derived from forcing cultures to copy each other or from registering their advance or decline against some hypothetically ideal scale. The record of their successive adaptations to their changing environments reveals the conditions under which cultures have developed and according to which they might be said to persist.

A BIBLIOGRAPHICAL ESSAY

IN WHAT FOLLOWS, I attempt an extended commentary on a number of works, mainly in Arabic, English, and French, that deal with the topics discussed in each chapter. I have highlighted works in Arabic and works by Muslim authors because these are usually underrepresented in bibliographies compiled by Western scholars. Many important works on classical Islamic culture are doubtless omitted. Furthermore, I have cited only those works that seemed to me to be important or interesting enough to require assessment. For a comprehensive bibliography on all things Islamic, the reader should consult Sauvaget-Cahen, *Introduction to The History of The Muslim East* (Berkeley: The University of California Press, 1965), although its coverage of cultural matters is relatively incomplete. For translations into English, see Margaret Anderson, *Arabic Materials in English Translation* (Boston: G. K. Hall, 1980), which is conveniently arranged under headings, viz., philosophy, science, literature, and so forth, and covers the classical and modern periods.

The translations of the Koran cited in the text are either my own or those of Arberry (see below, Chapter 2).

Chapter 1

Among various introductions to Islam, H. A. R. Gibb, *Mohammedanism* (London: Home University Library, 1949), has been a perennial favorite. It is an elegant and concise work but is now dated in several respects, most notably in its account of the origins of the various Islamic sciences. Much larger in size and spirit is M. G. S. Hodgson, *The Venture of Islam*, Vol. 1 (Chicago: The University of Chicago Press, 1974), a work that seeks to place Islamic culture within world history. Its numerous insights are enormously inspiring; its few faults of detail are easily overlooked. But it is not an introduction in the strict sense because it assumes some prior knowledge of Islam, and Hodgson's technical vocabulary is something of an obstacle to the beginner.

Three works by Muslim authors should be mentioned: F. Rahman, *Islam* (London: Weidenfield and Nicolson, 1966), a controversial work that attacks, *inter alia*, Muslim apologists and Western Orientalists but is particularly perceptive on Islamic philosophy and more informative than Gibb on Islamic modernism. S. H. Nasr, *Ideals and Realities of Islam* (London: George Allen and Unwin, 1966), was in origin a series of public lectures. The author is best known for his work on Islamic science but this work contains a number of illuminating insights, albeit with pronounced neo-Sufi sympathies. The bibliography contains many titles by Muslim authors. M. Arkoun, *La Pensée Arabe* (Paris: Presses Universitaires de France, 1975), is the most difficult but also the most rewarding of these works. The author owes much to the modern French schools of semeiology and cultural anthropology and seems at times to say much about Arab Islamic culture that applies to all other cultures; nonetheless, the analysis throughout is refreshingly different from the usual intellectual history of the Arabs (which is a processional of great minds), and seeks boldly to gather the social, economic, and intellectual strands.

Broader in scope are G. Von Grunebaum, *Medieval Islam*, 2nd. ed. (Chicago: The University of Chicago Press, 1961) and D. M. Dunlop, *Arab Civilization to A.D. 1500* (London: Longmans, 1971). The first sets out to "trace the temper and flavor of the Muslim Middle Ages" and, with frequent comparisons to Hellenistic and Persian cultures, carries the reader along by commenting on extensive and generally well chosen quotations from medieval authors. The book is marred, however, by an ever growing insistence on demonstrating the "stagnation" of Muslim culture. The second has no such axe to grind but tends to be a history of great minds rather than of the culture as a whole. But it is accurate and informative. P. Crone and M. A. Cook, *Hagarism* (Cambridge: Harvard University Press, 1977), argues interestingly but unconvincingly that Islam is a Judaic "heresy." The Hagarenes were "barbarians" who dismantled beautiful and orderly cultures and reconstituted them pell-mell. With Wansbrough (see below, Chapter 2) it shares a scepticism towards the early Islamic sources but waives this scepticism towards other traditions, e.g., Syriac.

Finally, the second half of Ibn Khaldūn's *Muqaddima* (corresponding to Vol. 2, pp. 409-463 and much of Vol. 3 of the Rosenthal translation) is a history of the rise and development of Islamic culture down to the author's own days in the early fifteenth century. It remains, quite simply, the best *muqaddima* to the subject.

Chapter 2

Of the various translations of the Koran, that by A. J. Arberry, *The Koran Interpreted* (London: Oxford University Press, 1975), remains, despite its archaisms, the best, combining accuracy with literary merit. Of translations by Muslims, that of Muhammed Ali, *The Holy Qur'ān* (Lahore: Ahmadiyya Press, 1951) is the best but is not as graceful as Arberry's. N. J. Dawood, *The Koran* (Harmondsworth: Penguin Books, 1956), is readable but takes too many liberties with the text.

Of the half-dozen major classical commentaries on the Koran, very little has been translated into English. W. M. Watt, *Bell's Intoduction to the Qur'ān* (Edinburgh: University Press, 1970), is good on the history and structure of the Koran, and the notes contain a valuable bibliography, but it is not a work of interpretation in the fullest sense.

The work of J. Wansbrough, *Quranic Studies* (London: Oxford University Press, 1977) is an attempt at "higher criticism" of the Koran and currently an influential voice in Koran interpretation. However, it rejects all tradition before the ninth century as "symbolic," "personification," or, quite simply, "ingenuous," and it identifies Islam with an almost exclusively Judaic terminological framework as being the most satisfying cultural parallel. The essential research of N. Abbott, *Studies in Arabic Literary Papyri II* (Chicago: The University of Chicago Press, 1967), and F. Sezgin, *Geschichte des Arabischen Schrifttums 1* (Leiden: Brill, 1967), on the genesis of Koranic exegesis is too curtly dismissed by Wansbrough.

Among modern Muslim interpreters, Muhammad Arkoun holds most promise: see, e.g., "Lecture de la Sourate 18" in *Annales E.S.C.* (August, 1980). M. Khalfallāh, *Al-Fann al-Qiṣaṣī fi ʾl Qurʾān* ("Narrative Art in the Koran") (Cairo: Anglo-Egyptian, 1965), caused a great stir when it first appeared in 1949 for arguing that the Koran is best interpreted as a literary rather than a historical work. But it is repetitive and stilted in style.

Chapter 3

For translations of *Ḥadīth*, see Glossary, s.v. Bukhārī, Muslim. On the genesis of the *Ḥadīth*, the works of Abbott and Sezgin cited above are fundamental.

There is no comprehensive study of the structure and the function of the *Ḥadīth*. I. Goldziher, *Muslim Studies*, Vol. 2 (Albany: SUNY Press, 1968-72), is a scholarly introduction but now dated in some of its major conclusions and is in any case historical in approach. A. Guillaume, *The Traditions of Islam* (Beirut: Khayats reprints, 1966) is basically a history of the *Ḥadīth* but is unduly critical of its authenticity and over-emphasizes the importance of *isnād*.

Of the many lives of Muhammad currently in print, that by W. M. Watt, *Muhammad, Prophet and Statesman* (London: Oxford University Press, 1969) is probably still the best. It abbreviates the author's two earlier volumes, *Muhammad at Mecca* (Oxford: Clarendon Press, 1953) and *Muhammad at Medina* (Oxford: Clarendon Press, 1956), generally praised for their grasp of the social structure of the period. The older work of Sir W. Muir, *The Life of Mohammad* (Edinburgh: John Grant, 1923), accurately reconstructs the original sources but is virulently anti-Islamic. Maxime Rodinson, *Mohammed* (London: Allen Lane, 1971), mixes an unsatisfactory psychological approach with a convincing sociological analysis. But given the Marxism of the author, there are few Marxist insights. A. Guillaume, *The Life of Muhammad* (London: Oxford University Press, 1955), is a translation of the eighth-century life of the Prophet by Ibn Isḥāq; it is the earliest surviving biography and makes difficult reading but is the starting point for any serious study of the Prophet's life. Of lives by Muslims, that by Muhammad Ḥusayn Haykal, *Ḥayāt Muḥammad*, 3rd ed. (Cairo: Dār al-Kutub, 1358/1939; frequently reprinted), has had much influence. Haykal emphasizes the humanity, simplicity, and nobility of Muḥammad, but the work is heavily apologetic.

On *Fiqh*, the works of J. Schacht, *Introduction to Islamic Law* (London: Oxford University Press, 1964), and the earlier and more specialized *Origins of Muhammadan Jurisprudence* (Oxford: Clarendon Press, 1953), are still fundamental, although N. Abbott, as noted above, has criticized Schacht's views on the *Ḥadīth*. Easier to read and just as scholarly is N. Coulson, *A History of Islamic Law* (Edinburgh: University Press, 1964). Schacht's approach is historical, Coulson's is more legal. Shāfiᶜī's important epistle on jurisprudence has been translated by Majid Khadduri, *Islamic Jurisprudence; Shāfiᶜī's Risāla* (Baltimore: Johns Hopkins Press, 1961). Of works by modern Muslims, S. Mahmassani, *The Philosophy of Jurisprudence in Islam*, translated by F. Ziadeh (Leiden: Brill, 1961), is broader than its title for it provides an introduction to Islamic law that combines historical scholarship with the acumen of an experienced lawyer. Its commentary on the *majalla*, the nineteenth-century Ottoman civil code based on the *Sharīᶜa*, is especially valuable for students of modern Islamic law.

On the history of the Islamic judiciary, the work of E. Tyan, *Histoire de l'organisation judiciaire en pays d'Islam* (Leiden: Brill, 1960), is masterly but a shade too long. On the sociology of Islamic law the French Orientalists have done pioneering work: see, e.g., R. Brunschvig, "Urbanisme Medieval et droit musulman," *Revue d'Études Islamiques* 15 (1947); *idem*, "Considerations sociologiques sur le droit musulman ancien," *Studia Islamica*, 3 (1955), and G. H. Bousquet, *Du droit musulman et de son application effective dans le monde* (Algiers, 1949).

Chapter 4

There are several anthologies of *Adab*. That by Eric Schroeder, *Muhammad's People* (Portland, Maine: Bond Wheelwright, 1955), is admirable in its selections and style, rendering verse and prose with equal grace. Other anthologies include A. J. Arberry, *Aspects of Islamic Civilization* (London: George Allen, 1964), but the extended commentaries detract from continuous reading and the selections are of unequal merit. W. H. McNeill and M. Waldman, *The Islamic World* (New York: Oxford University Press, 1973) brings in Persian and Turkish selections and is better arranged than B. Lewis, *Islam*, 2 vols. (New York: Harper & Row, 1974), which is too fragmentary. J. Kritzeck, *Anthology of Islamic Literature* (Harmondsworth: Penguin Books, 1964) has some interesting selections.

With regard to studies of Arabic literature, H. A. R. Gibb, *Arabic Literature*, 2nd. ed. (Oxford: Clarendon Press, 1966) is a brief and elegant introduction but not very strong on textual analysis, and the divisions of Arab literary history into ages of "heroism," of "gold," and then of "silver" betray a nostalgia that is not really warranted. A. Hamori, *On the Art of Medieval Arabic Literature* (Princeton: Princeton University Press, 1975), applies some contemporary theories of literary criticism to Arabic poetry with fruitful results but is more difficult to read than Gibb and more restricted in scope. In Arabic, the works of Zakī Mubārak, *Al-Nathr al-fannī fī al-Qarn al-Rābiᶜ* ("Literary Prose in the Fourth Century") (Cairo: al-Maktaba al-Tijāriyya, 1957), and Shawqī Ḍayf, *al-ᶜAṣr al-ᶜAbbāsī al-Awwal* ("The First Abbasid Age") (Cairo: Dār al-Maᶜārif, 1966) are most valuable, although restricted in subject.

Surprisingly, there has been no large-scale or systematic study of Jāḥiẓ since C. Pellat, *Le Milieu Basrien et La Formation de Gāḥiẓ* (Paris: Maison-Neuve, 1953). For an excellent selection from his works, C. Pellat, *The Life and Works of Jahiz* (London: Routledge, 1969), provides the best introduction to this thinker.

Chapter 5

On Arabic Islamic historiography, the genesis of the genre is best dealt with in N. Abbott, *Studies in Arabic Literary Papyri I* (Chicago: The University of Chicago Press, 1957), and in A. Dūrī, *Baḥth fī Nashʾat ᶜilm al-taʾrīkh ᶜind al-ᶜArab* ("A Study of the Origins of Arabic Historiography") (Beirut: Catholic Press, 1960). Both are works of meticulous scholarship. F. Rosenthal, *A History of Muslim Historiography*, 2nd ed. (Leiden: Brill, 1968), and Shākir Muṣṭafā, *Al-Tārīkh al-ᶜArabī waʾl Muʾarrikhūn* ("Arab History and Historians"), Vol. 1 (Beirut: Dār al-ᶜilm liʾl Malāyīn, 1978), have a similar plan and treatment. Both tend to the "catalogue" style, especially the latter work, and to a certain superficiality where some individual historians are concerned. But the data in both is plentiful and, on the whole, accurate. Certain periods and figures in historiography are dealt with in B. Lewis and P. M. Holt, eds., *Historians of the Middle East* (London: Oxford University Press, 1962).

An anthology of Arab historical thought is an urgent desideratum. Only a few of the major classical historians have been translated into English. See the bibliography in Gibb, *Arabic Literature*, and Anderson, *Arabic Materials*; see also T. Khalidi, *Islamic Historiography* (Albany: SUNY Press, 1975), and A. Shboul, *Al-Masᶜūdi and His World* (London: Ithaca Press, 1979). The first assesses him primarily as a thinker; the second primarily as a source.

Chapter 6

There are two brief and sensitive introductions to Sufism: R. A. Nicholson, *The Mystics of Islam* (Beirut: Khayats reprints, 1966; reproduces the 1914 edition), and A. J. Arberry, *Sufism* (London: George Allen, 1950). Both were scholars who were able to share in the Sufi mood to varying degrees. The first work is less historically structured and more impressionistic; the second is too intent upon picturing Sufism as a story of progressive decline.

An Islamicist who left a great impact on both Europe and the Arab

Islamic world was Louis Massignon, whose work on Sufism, primarily *La Passion d'al-Hallaj*, 2nd ed. (Paris: Vrin, 1954), and *Essai sur les origines du lexique technique de la mystique musulmane* (Paris: Geughner, 1922), are unrivalled in their re-creation of the Sufi spirit. See also Hodgson, *The Venture*, 1:392 ff.

The anthology of M. Smith, *Readings from the Mystics of Islam* (London: Luzac, 1950) is an admirable short selection, arranged chronologically. The translation is particularly good, and there are brief biographical notes on each Sufi. The introduction to Sufism by al-Kalābādhī (d. 990) has been translated by A. J. Arberry, *The Doctrine of the Sufis* (Cambridge: Harvard University Press, 1930), and provides an early medieval scholar's compendium of Sufi views, stressing Sufi orthodoxy.

On the Sufi orders, J. S. Trimingham, *The Sufi Orders in Islam* (Oxford: Clarendon Press, 1971) is a useful historical survey but too thin on the socio-political role of the orders. Trimingham's bibliography and glossary are comprehensive. The work of modern anthropologists on the orders has yielded valuable insights: see, e.g., M. Gilsenan, *Saint and Sufi in Modern Egypt* (Oxford: Clarendon Press, 1973).

Chapter 7

On Islamic theology and philosophy in general the clearest and briefest introduction is M. Mahdi, "Islamic Theology and Philosophy," *Encyclopaedia Britannica* (1974). It takes the story up to the nineteenth century. W. M. Watt, *Islamic Philosophy and Theology* (Edinburgh: University Press, 1964) makes a number of valuable points and attempts to investigate the social context but his emphasis on the influence of Greek philosophy is too strong and his views on the origins of some movements are to be treated with caution. More in touch with the sources is Watt's earlier work, *Free-Will and Predestination in Early Islam* (London: Luzac, 1948). A. J. Wensinck, *The Muslim Creed* (Cambridge: University Press, 1932), is a basic work on early theology because of the author's exhaustive knowledge of the *Ḥadīth*. L. Gardet and G. Anawati, *Introduction à la Theologie Musulmane* (Paris: Vrin, 1948), is a good survey of Sunnite theology stressing the importance of the Koran and the *Ḥadīth* in the rise of Islamic theology. I. Goldziher, *Le Dogme et la loi de l'Islam* (Paris, 1958), is an older work but still of much value, although it tends to be abrupt in characterizing some theological movements as "orthodox" and others as "unorthodox."

On early theology, the works and articles of Josef van Ess and Wilfred Madelung are fundamental. Their articles can be traced through J. S. Pearson, *Index Islamicus* (Cambridge: Heffer, 1958, and Supplements). Of particular importance for early developments are J. van Ess, *Anfänge muslimischer Theologie* (Beirut/Wiesbaden: Fritz Steiner, 1977), and W. Madelung, *Der Imam al-Qasim ibn Ibrahim* (Berlin: de Gruyter, 1965). On Muᶜtazilism, the article by H. S. Nyberg, "Muᶜtazila," *The Encyclopaedia of Islam* (1st ed.), is still valuable, although wrong on their political connections. G. F. Hourani, *Islamic Rationalism: The Ethics of ʿAbd al-Jabbar* (Oxford: Clarendon Press, 1971), devoted to a major Muʿtazilite figure, deals lucidly with many aspects of Muʿtazilite thought. On Ashʿarī and Ashʿarism, see M. Allard, *Le Problème des Attributs Divins dans la doctrine d'al-Ashʿarī* (Beirut: Catholic Press, 1965), and J. Bouma, *Le Conflit autour du Coran* (Amsterdam: J. Van Campen, 1959). Both are detailed and perceptive studies of basic problems in Islamic theology. For translations, see glossary, s.v. Ashʿarī.

On Islamic philosophy, the most lucid introduction is R. Walzer, "The Rise of Islamic Philosophy," *Oriens* 3 (1950). His various studies of the subject are assembled in R. Walzer, *Greek into Arabic* (Cambridge: Harvard University Press, 1962) and his insights and interpretations remain fundamental. Two historical surveys should be mentioned: Majid Fakhry, *A History of Islamic Philosophy* (New York: Columbia University Press, 1970), and M. M. Sharif, ed., *A History of Muslim Philosophy*, 2 vols. (Wiesbaden: Harrassowitz, 1963-66), and one collection of recent studies, G. Hourani, ed., *Essays on Islamic Philosophy and Science* (Albany: SUNY Press, 1975). For translations, see the Glossary, s.v. Fārābī, Ibn Rushd, Ibn Sīnā and Kindī, and also Anderson, *Arabic Materials*.

Two translations have especially valuable introductions: M. Mahdi, *Alfarabi's Philosophy of Plato and Aristotle*, revised ed. (Ithaca: Cornell University Press, 1969), which has two valuable introductions to Fārābī's philosophy, and G. F. Hourani, *Averroes on the Harmony of Religion and Philosophy* (London: Luzac, 1976), which has an excellent introduction to the background and views of Ibn Rushd.

Chapter 8

Two good introductory surveys are G. Anawati, "Science," in Holt, Lambton, Lewis, eds., *The Cambridge History of Islam,* Vol. 2 (Cambridge: Cambridge University Press, 1970), and Chapter X in J. Schacht and C. E. Bosworth, eds., *The Legacy of Islam*, 2nd ed. (Oxford: Clarendon Press, 1974), by several authors. This latter work has a workable bibliography. S. H. Nasr, *An Introduction to Islamic Cosmological Doctrines* (Cambridge: Harvard University Press, 1964), is, I believe, this author's best work and deals with diverse issues in Islamic science. F. Rosenthal, *The Classical Heritage in Islam* (London: Routledge, 1975), includes translations from several scientists. The various articles by P. Kraus are of great importance and can be traced through the *Index Islamicus*.

On medicine, the short introduction by M. Ulmann, *Islamic Medicine* (Edinburgh: University Press, 1978), is readable and informative, but the accent is on medical literature rather than practice. The various articles of M. Meyerhoff, traceable through the *Index Islamicus*, range over a wide spectrum of topics in Islamic medicine. On the concept of scientific progress, see T. Khalidi, "The Idea of Progress in Classical Islam," *Journal of Near Eastern Studies*, 40 (1981).

On classical geography, the starting point is S. Maqbul Ahmad, "Djughrāfiya," in *Encyclopaedia of Islam*, 2nd ed. This article surveys the geographical literature and many of its major figures and theories. The author has done much valuable work in the field, and his articles can be traced through the *Index Islamicus*. More extensive is I. Krachkovskii, *Tārīkh al-Adab al-Jughrāfī al-ʿArabī* ("History of Arab Geographical Literature"), 2 vols. translated by S. Hāshim (Cairo: Lujnat al-Taʾlīf, 1957), the standard work in the field and a work of careful scholarship, although it tends to read like a catalogue in certain parts. His bibliography is massive. Islamic geographical ideas are discussed with much perception by scholars such as A. Miquel, *La Géographie humaine du monde musulman* (Paris, La Haye: Mouton, 1967), and A. Shboul, *Al-Masʿūdī and His World.*

A summary of classical Islamic theories of geography may be found in A. Jwaideh, trans., *The Introductory Chapters of Yāqūt's Muʿjam al-Buldān* (Leiden: Brill, 1959). Yāqūt (d. 1229) is the author of two celebrated geographical dictionaries.

Chapter 9

All three streams of Islamic political thought *(falsafī, sharʿī, adabī)* are treated in E. I. J. Rosenthal, *Political Thought in Medieval Islam* (Cambridge: Cambridge University Press, 1958). Rosenthal's work is criticized in A. S. Bin ʿAbd al-ʿĀlī, *al-Falsafa al-Siyāsiyya ʿind al-Fārābī* ("Farabi's Political Philosophy") (Beirut: Dār al-Talīʿa, 1979), a work of considerable subtlety, which stresses Fārābī's independence from the Greeks and the centrality of politics and of the Islamic environment in his philosophical views. Nāṣīf Naṣṣār, "Mafhūm al-umma fī falsafat al-Fārābī" ("The Definition of ʾUmma in Fārābī's Philosophy") in *Dirāsāt ʿArabiyya*, no. 6 (1976), provides an illuminating analysis of Fārābī's use of this crucial political term. M. Mahdi and R. Lerner, *Medieval Political Philosophy* (Glencoe: Free Press, 1963), translates selections from Muslim political philosophers.

On political theory of the *sharʿi* kind, T. W. Arnold, *The Caliphate* (Oxford: Clarendon Press, 1924), discusses the theory and history of this institution. Māwardī's importance has been highlighted in Gibb, "Al-Māwardī's Theory of the Khilāfah," in *Islamic Culture*, 11 (1937). See also Gibb, "Some Considerations on the Sunni Theory of the Caliphate," in Shaw and Polk, eds., *Studies in the Civilization of Islam* (Boston: Beacon Press, 1962). On Ghazālī, see L. Binder, "Al-Ghazali's Theory of Islamic Government," *Muslim World,* 45 (1955). On later theory, see H. Laoust, *Essai sur les doctrines sociales et politiques de Ibn Tamiyya* (Cairo: IFAO, 1939), a work of painstaking scholarship. There is a good anthology of *sharʿī* political thought in Y. Ibish, *Nuṣūṣ al-fikr al-siyāsī al-islāmī* ("Readings in Islamic Political Thought) (Beirut: Dār al-Ṭalīʿa, 1966). This deals with Sunnite doctrines and of the imāmate and deserves translation.

On *adabī* political thought, see A. Lambton, "Islamic Political Thought," in Schacht and Bosworth, *The Legacy of Islam*, somewhat sweeping in its judgments but has a workable bibliography, which cites three important articles by the author on *adabī* political thought. For translations, see, e.g., H. Darke, *The Book of Government* (London: Routledge, 1960), that is, Niẓām al-Mulk's *Siyaset-Nameh*; the celebrated work on Abbasid court etiquette by Hilāl al-Ṣābī (d. 1056) in E. Salem, *Rusūm Dār al-Khilāfah: The Rules and Regulations of The Abbasid Court* (Beirut: AUB Press, 1977), and the famous work of Ibn al-Ṭiqṭaqā (d. ca. 1262) in C. E. J. Whitting, *Al-Fakhri On The System of Government and The Muslim Dynasties* (London: Luzac, 1947).

Chapter 10

The most recent and most comprehensive study of Ibn Khaldūniana is in Aziz al-Azmeh, *Ibn Khaldūn in Modern Scholarship* (London: Third World Center, 1981). This provides a critique (often fierce) of various interpretations of Ibn Khaldūn and is valuable, especially for its emphasis on Ibn Khaldūn's *History* as opposed to his *Muqaddima*, as well as for a comprehensive and annotated bibliography of studies on Ibn Khaldūn, which lists 854 items. Azmeh's own interpretation of Ibn Khaldūn is in his *Ibn Khaldūn, An Essay in Reinterpretation* (London: Cass, 1981), which situates his thought within the dominant sciences of his day and reduces the Aristotelian dimension to only one factor in the structure of his thought, rather than to the dominant factor as argued in M. Mahdi, *Ibn Khaldūn's Philosophy of History* (Chicago: The University of Chicago Press, 1964). This latter work, however, remains, despite Azmeh's critique, fundamental. A recent and perceptive examination of Ibn Khaldūn is in M. A. al-Jābirī, *Al-ʿAṣabiyya waʾl Dawla* ("Solidarity and State") (Casablanca: Dār al-Thaqāfa, 1971), which seeks to analyze the totality of his thought, eschews the "modernization" of his theories, and has a valuable glossary of basic Ibn Khaldūnian terms.

For translations of Ibn Khaldūn's works, see Azmeh, *Ibn Khaldūn in Modern Scholarship*, pp. 245 ff.

Chapter 11

The volume of work on the problem of the *turāth* grows larger every year. There is as yet no full-length study of this literature, in Arabic or any other language.

Those who emphasize a historical approach to the *turāth* include: Abdullah Laroui, *al-ʿArab waʾl Fikr al-tārīkhī* ("The Arabs and Historical Thought") (Beirut: Dār al-Ḥaqīqa, 1973). Laroui maintains that a historical understanding of *turāth* is the only way in which the Arabs can enrich world culture and not become simply its imitators. See also his article "Qaḍiyyat al-turāth wa'l inbi'āth al-ḥaḍārī" ("The Problem of *Turāth* and Cultural Renaissance") in *al-Fikr al-'Arabī al-mu'āṣir*, no. 12 (May, 1981). Arguing in much the same vein and showing clearly the influence of French theories of the sociology of knowledge is M. A. Jābirī, *Naḥnu wa'l Turāth* ("We and the Turāth") (Beirut: Dār al-Ṭalī'a, 1980). Jābirī argues that one must first understand the *turāth* in its specific environment before one proceeds to "exploit" it. N. Naṣṣār, *Ṭarīq al-istiqlāl al-falsafī* ("The Path to Philosophical Independence") (Beirut: Dār al-Ṭalī'a, 1975), asserts that the path to independence and originality of Arab thought lies through recognition of the unique historical situation of Arab Islamic culture. Anwar 'Abd al-Malik, *Dirāsāt fī al-Thaqāfa al-waṭaniyya* ("Studies in National Culture") (Beirut: Dār al-Ṭalī'a, 1967), laments the lack of a historical methodology and argues that the *turāth* should include not only Arab-Islamic but also the whole of Egyptian history. W. Sharāra, *al Mas'ala al-Tārīkhiyya fī al-fikr al-'Arabī alḥadīth* ("The Problem of History in Modern Arabic Thought") (Beirut: Ma'had al-Inmā', 1977), argues that most modern historiography is ideological and thus reveals more about the authors than about their subjects.

Less historically minded and eclectic in approach are such works as Zakī Najīb Maḥmūd, *al-Ma'qūl wa'llā Ma'qūl fī turāthinā al-fikrī* ("The Rational and the Irrational in Our Intellectual *Turāth*") (Beirut: Dār al-Shurūq, 1975) and *Tajdīd al-fikr al-'Arabī* ("Renewal of Arabic Thought") (Beirut: Dār al-Shurūq, 1973), which single out for special praise the "rationalists" of the *turāth*, i.e., the Mu'tazilites and Ibn Rushd, and stress their relevance to the modern theory and practice of freedom. Muḥammad 'Amāra, *Naẓra Jadīda ilā al-turāth* ("A New Examination of the *Turāth*") (Beirut: al-Mu'assasa al-'Arabiyya, 1974) selects from the *turāth* its "progressive" elements, i.e., those elements that emphasize free will and "a revolutionary" mentality. The heroes, here too, are the Mu'tazilites and the philosophers. Adonis, *al-Thābit wa'l Mutaḥawwil* ("The Changeless and The Changing"), Vol. 1 (Beirut: Dār al-'Awda, 1974), praises the "Progressives" but goes further than most in attacking the "reactionaries" of the Arab Islamic *turāth*. Ḥ. Ḥanafī, *al-Turāth wa'l Tajdīd* ("*Turāth* and Renewal") (Beirut: Dār al-Tanwīr, 1981), intends to harness the *turāth* in the service of "the masses" and of "liberation" by liberating it from all its "negative" elements, e.g., its "myths," "hero-worship," and "magic."

Diverse Marxist viewpoints are represented in such works as Maḥmūd Amīn al-'Ālim, *al-Thaqāfa wa'l Thawra* ("Culture and Revolution") (Beirut: Dār al-Ādāb, 1970), which sees the *turāth* as part of a wider struggle for a more humane, open, and progressive society and finding in religious values no contradiction with socialism, provided belief does not lead to predestinarianism or intellectual repression. Al-Ṭayyib Tīʾinī, *Min al-Turāth ilā al-Thawra* ("From *Turāth* to Revolution"), Vol. 1 (Beirut: Dār Ibn Khaldūn, 1976), is a rigidly Marxist analysis of *turāth* purporting to show how at each historical stage various classes spawned various ideologies and arguing for a selective attitude picking out "progressive" *turāth* as a path to Arab revolution. Aḥmad ʿUlabī, *al-Islām waʾl Manhaj al-Tārīkhī* ("Islam and Historical Method") (Beirut: Dār al-Ṭalīʿa, 1975), warns against the abuse of *turāth* for political purposes and against revolutionizing it artificially, and maintains that the investigation of *turāth* is a job for academics lest it be abused by reactionaries to further class interests. Mahdī ʿĀmil, *Azmat al-ḥadāra al-ʿArabiyya am azmat al-burjuwāziyyāt al-ʿArabiyya?* ("Is It a Crisis of Arab Culture or of The Arab Bourgeoisie?") (Beirut: Dār al-Fārābī, 1974) affirms that the *turāth* is not the cause but the effect of regression. The question for him is not our view of the past but the specific historical form of its expression in the present. We must neither revive nor suppress the *turāth* but "possess it scientifically," the job of the Arab proletariat.

More explicitly Islamic are such works as Sayyid Quṭb, *Fī al-Tārīkh: Fikra wa minhāj* ("On History: A Theory and a Method") (Beirut: Dār al-Shurūq, 1974). Islam is described as creative, action-oriented, and universal, and Islamic history must be written by Muslims in order to point out the role of Islam in world history.

Two writers who may be called "Islamic Marxists" are ʿAbd al-Raḥmān al-Sharqāwī, *Qirāʾāt fī al-fikr al-Islāmī* ("Readings in Islamic Thought") (Beirut: Dār al-Waṭan al-ʿArabī, 1975), and Hādī al-ʿAlawī, *Fī al-Dīn waʾl Turāth* ("On Religion and *Turāth*") (Beirut: Dār al-Ṭalīʿa, 1973). The first argues that Islam carries within itself the elements of its revival and sees in it perennial qualities of greatness and revolutionary justice, e.g., that Islam has always called for national ownership of the major means of production. The second maintains that the socialist and democratic elements of Islamic *turāth*, long hidden from us by imperialists and reactionaries, are those most worthy of revival.

GLOSSARY OF ARABIC PROPER NAMES AND TERMS

THIS GLOSSARY gives biographical notices of certain names and terms (indicated with an asterisk*) not sufficiently identified in the text and, where appropriate, references to English translations deemed helpful. For more detailed information, the reader should consult the *Encyclopaedia of Islam* or similar references.

ABBASIDS (750-1258): Second, and longest lasting, dynasty of Arabic Islamic history. Their political power began to wane ca. 850, but the capital they founded, Baghdad, remained a vital cultural center throughout their rule. In origin the *shīʿa* (party) of ʿAbbās, uncle of the Prophet, and thus part of the revolutionary loyalist parties, the Abbasids eventually veered closer to Sunnism in matters of faith.

ʿABD AL-ḤAMĪD AL-KĀTIB (d. 750): State secretary of the last Umayyad caliph and one of the early figures of secretarial *Adab*, associated in outlook, style, and friendship with Ibn al-Muqaffaʿ (q.v.). His few surviving epistles are elegant, sophisticated, and epigrammatical, and betray the concern of early *Adab* writers with Byzantine and Persian culture.

ABŪ BAKR (d. 634): One of Muḥammad's very earliest converts, he became his closest supporter and confidant and eventually his first deputy or *khalīfa* (caliph), and head of the Muslim state. His piety and statesmanship made him one of Islam's most revered personalities. Abū Bakr unified Arabia under Islam and launched the conquests outside it.

ABŪ YAʿLĀ (d. 1065): Celebrated Ḥanbalite, i.e., follower of Ibn Ḥanbal, (q.v.), jurist, teacher, and chief judge of Baghdad, he reformed the judiciary corps and thus gained direct experience of government affairs. His treatise on politics *(al-Aḥkām al-Sulṭāniyya)* was the major Ḥanbalite statement on the theory of government in classical Islam.

ʿALĪ (d. 660): Cousin and son-in-law of the Prophet and fourth caliph, he inspired little loyalty during his own troubled life, but was revered after his death. He is second only to the Prophet in spiritual importance, wisdom, and virtue.

ASHʿARĪ (d. 935): Foremost theologian of Sunnī Islam and enemy of the Muʿtazila. He was an heresiographer and polemicist. Several of his treatises have been translated into English; see especially R. J. McCarthy, *The Theology of al-Ashʿarī* (Beirut: Librairie Orientale, 1953).

ᶜAṬṬĀR (d. 1229): A Sufi master from Khurāsān, he began his life as a druggist. Then he embraced Sufism and spent his last years in secluded contemplation. For a sample of his work in translation, see Margaret Smith, *Readings from The Mystics of Islam* (London: Luzac, 1972), pp. 80-91.

BUKHĀRĪ (d. 870): Editor, with Muslim (q.v.), of one of the two most authoritative *(Ṣaḥīḥ)* collections of the *Ḥadīth*. He is reputed to have made his selection of 7,000 *Ḥadīths* from a total of about half a million amassed through wide travelling and a prodigous memory. Bukhārī's *Ṣaḥīḥ* has enjoyed an eminence second only to the Koran in Sunni Islam. There is a partial translation of the *Ṣaḥīḥ* by Muhammad Asad (Lahore, 1938). There are also lengthy extracts in Arthur Jeffery, ed., *A Reader On Islam* (s'-Gravenhage: Mouton, 1962), and in Muhammad Ali, *A Manual of Ḥadīth*, 2nd ed. (London: Curzon Press, 1978).

BUYID DYNASTY (945-1055): The first in a series of military non-Arab dynasties to have taken the Abbasids of Baghdad under their wing. The Buyid dynasty was close to Shīᶜism, ruling over a Sunnite population, and followed a generally tolerant cultural and religious policy.

FĀRĀBĪ (d. 950): Foremost Muslim philosopher of the Aristotelian school, he was a native of Turkestan and spent most of his life in Baghdad, Damascus, and Aleppo, in the last of which he was a member of the ruler's court. Many of his extant writings have been translated into English; see especially Muhsin Mahdi, *Alfarabi's Philosophy of Plato and Aristotle* (Ithaca, NY: Cornell University Press, 1969).

GHAZĀLĪ (d. 1111): Sufi, theologian, jurist, religious reformer, he was one of Islam's most original intellects. Born in Khurāsān, he taught at Baghdad, travelled widely, and died at his own Sufi retreat in Khurāsān. His fame was already well established in his lifetime, and he was well known to the great political and religious figures of his day. Much of his work has been translated into English; see especially his autobiography, W. M. Watt, *The Faith and Practice of al-Ghazālī* (London: Allen and Unwin, 1953).

AL-ḤALLĀJ (d. 922): Arguably the most interesting of the early Sufis, Al-Ḥallāj alternately baffled and entranced his contemporaries with his utterances and his lifestyle. He was imprisoned and later crucified in Baghdad. Some of his utterances are translated in Eric Schroeder's *Muḥammad's People* (Portland, Maine: Wheelwright, 1955).

ḤASAN OF BAṢRA (d. 728): Born in Medina, he lived in Basra. Ḥasan was a towering religious figure of Islam's first century. He was a "patron saint" of both Sufism and theology. Short extracts of his sayings are translated in Margaret Smith, *Readings*. His letter to the caliph ᶜUmar II is translated in W. H. McNeill and M. Waldman, *The Islamic World* (New York: Oxford University Press, 1973), pp. 79-81.

AL-HUJWĪRĪ (d. 1072): Born in Afghanistan, he died at Lahore. Al-Hujwīrī travelled widely and met many of the prominent Sufis of his age. His work manifests an interest in the theoretical and institutional aspects of Sufism. See the translation of his principal work in R. A. Nicholson, *Kashf al-Maḥjūb* (London: Luzac, 1911).

IBN AL-ʿARABĪ (d. 1240): One of the greatest figures of classical Sufism, he was known as "The Great Master." Born in Spain, he travelled to Egypt, Iraq, Asia Minor, and finally settled in Damascus. See the translation of Ibn al-ʿArabī's *Tarjumān al-Ashwāq* by R. A. Nicholson (London: Oriental Translation Fund, 1911).

IBN ḤANBAL (d. 855): A major figure of classical Islamic jurisprudence and founder of the Ḥanbalite school of law, one of the four Sunni schools, he was born in Baghdad, where he led an active life of teaching. He was imprisoned and flogged by the caliphs for his anti-Muʿtazilite views. Restored to favor before the end of his life, Ibn Ḥanbal had an enormous popular following. He is best known for his *Musnad*, a collection of the *Ḥadīth* arranged according to *isnād*; his conservative views made him an enemy of all rationalistic theology and an advocate of the primacy of the Koran and the *Ḥadīth* as sources of law.

IBN JAMĀʿA (d. 1333): A prominent Mamluk (q.v.), jurist, and judge, he came from a noted scholarly family of Jerusalem and was judge of Jerusalem and, later, chief judge of Cairo and Damascus. There is a summary of the main arguments of his work in political theory in E. I. J. Rosenthal, *Political Thought in Medieval Islam* (Cambridge: Cambridge University Press, 1958), pp. 43-51.

IBN AL-MUQAFFAʿ (d. 757): A seminal figure in the development of Arabic literary and "secretarial" prose, Ibn al-Muqaffaʿ was of Persian origin and served in the chancery of Abbasid caliphs. He is said to have been executed for heresy by a caliph intent upon demonstrating Orthodoxy. Ibn al-Muqaffaʿ is best known for *Kalīla wa Dimna*, a collection of animal fables derived from Indian models, and for other epistles on *Adab*. There is an old transation of *Kalīla wa Dimna* by W. Knatchbull, *Kalīla and Dimna* (London: J. Parker, 1819). See also the lengthy excerpt in A. J. Arberry, *Aspects of Islamic Civilization* (London: Allen and Unwin, 1964).

IBN RUSHD (AVERROES) (d. 1198): Foremost Islamic philosopher of the Aristotelian school, Ibn Rushd was born in Cordoba of a family of jurists and became chief judge of his native city, falling out of, and then being restored to, favor with the regime. In addition to his commentaries on Aristotle, for which he was best known in the medieval West, he also wrote on medicine and law. Many of his works have been translated into English; see especially G. F. Hourani, *Averroes On the Harmony of Religion and Philosophy* (London: Luzac, 1976).

IBN SĪNĀ (AVICENNA) (d. 1037): Encyclopedic philosopher whose system combined Aristotelian with neo-Platonic elements, he was born near Bukhārā. Ibn Sīnā won renown with the rulers of his age as a physician, and he wrote voluminously on natural science, philosophy, medicine, and mysticism. For his autobiography, see W. E. Gohlman, *The Life of Ibn Sīnā* (Albany, NY: SUNY Press, 1974). Of special interest, too, is the translation of Ibn Sīnā's discussion of the soul in F. Rahman, *Avicenna's Psychology* (London: Oxford University Press, 1952).

IBN TAYMIYYA (d. 1328): Jurist, theologian, and religious reformer, he was born at Ḥarrān and lived in Damascus, where he quickly attained eminence as a Ḥanbalite scholar, lived a stormy life, and engaged in polemics against a wide spectrum of opponents. Although a Ḥanbalite, he was very independent in his judgments and deeply grounded in a wide variety of sciences, religious and non-religious alike. See the translation of a legal epistle in Omar Farrukh, *Ibn Taimiyya on Public and Private Law in Islam* (Beirut: Khayats, 1966).

ISMĀᶜĪLIS: A branch of Shīᶜism, Ismailism made its revolutionary debut late in the ninth century and succeeded in establishing various foci of power in diverse Islamic lands, most notably the Fatimid Caliphate in Egypt and Syria (tenth to twelfth centuries), the Qarmatians of Bahrain, and the Assassins of Persia and Syria. Ismailism was not a centralized political movement but did produce a rich corpus of thought with distinct neo-Platonic and Indian influences. The most famous cultural legacy of the Ismāᶜīlīs is the tenth-century encyclopedia known as the *Epistles of the Brethren of Purity*, a brief extract of which is translated in F. Rosenthal, *The Classical Heritage in Islam* (London: Routledge, 1975).

JĀBIR (fl. mid-eighth century): To this semi-legendary founder of Arab alchemy is attributed a diverse corpus of later writings dating probably from the tenth century and betraying Greek and Ismāᶜīlī influences. Extracts from the Jābir corpus are translated in F. Rosenthal, *The Classical Heritage in Islam.*

JĀḤIẒ (d. 869): Man of letters, humanist, and Muᶜtazilite theologian, Jāḥiẓ was arguably the most original intellect of classical Islam. Born in Baṣra, he lived in Baghdad, where he was close to the court. He wrote some 200 works varying in size from short epistles to multi-volume tomes. The most accessible introduction to his work is Charles Pellat, *The Life and Works of Jāḥiẓ* (London: Routledge, 1969), which contains translations of well-selected texts.

KINDĪ (d. ca. 866): First major figure of Islamic philosophy, Kindī was born in Kufa but settled in Baghdad as a young man, where he soon became close to a number of enlightened Abbasid caliphs, but fell out of favor when a policy of reaction set in. Kindī wrote on a wide variety of philosophical and scientific subjects and was close to Mu[c]tazilism. See the translation of his treatise on metaphysics in A. L. Ivry, *Al-Kindi's Metaphysics* (Albany, NY: SUNY Press, 1974).

MAMLUK EMPIRE (1250-1517): This empire was ruled by a military élite of Turkish, Mongol, and Circassian ex-slaves, where supreme power was held more often by strong men than by dynasties. The capital of the Mamluk Empire was Cairo, and at the height of its power, the Mamluks controlled lands from the Sudan to Asia Minor and from North Africa to the borders of Iraq.

MĀWARDĪ (d. 1058): Author of the most widely quoted treatise on political theory in Sunni Islam, Māwardī was raised in Basra and eventually settled in Baghdad. He was also a judge in Khurāsān and was used on diplomatic missions by the Buyids (q.v.). Apart from jurisprudence, Māwardī had wide cultural interests, which included *Adab* and theology. There is a summary of Māwardī's work on government in F. Rosenthal, *Political Thought,* pp. 27-37.

MEDINA: An oasis town about 325 kilometers north of Mecca, Medina encompassed, along with Mecca and Ṭā'if, the three leading towns of the Hijāz (or northwestern Arabia) on the eve of Islam. From 622 to 632, Medina was the Prophet's capital and, until about 656, the capital of the Arab empire also.

MU[c]ĀWIYA (d. 680): Founder of the Umayyad (q.v.) dynasty, Mu[c]āwiya and his family had embraced Islam late but quickly made themselves useful to the Muslim state as administrators, governors, and generals. Mu[c]āwiya was governor of Syria when he challenged [c]Alī (q.v.) successfully for supreme power. As caliph, Mu[c]āwiya was shrewd and tolerant, establishing the dynasty as an alliance between the ruling house and prominent Arab chieftains through whom centralization was effected from the new capital, Damascus.

MUSLIM (d. 875): Editor, with Bukhārī (q.v.), of one of the two most authoritative *(ṣaḥīḥ)* collections of the *Ḥadīth* in Sunni Islam, Muslim was born and died in Naisābūr. Like Bukhārī, he was a great traveller and is said to have made his final selection from a total of some 300,000 *Ḥadīths* that he collected. See the translation of the *Ṣaḥīḥ* by A. H. Siddiqi (Lahore, 1973).

NIẒĀM AL-MULK (d. 1092): Celebrated vizier of the early Seljuq (q.v.) Empire and author of *Siyāsat-nāmah* (Book of Government), Niẓām al-Mulk was for many years the real power behind the throne. He was a patron of scholarship and the founder of a number of colleges *(madrasa)* bearing his name. See the translation of *Siyāsat-nāmah* in H. Darke, *The Book of Government* (London: Routledge, 1960).

SELJUQ EMPIRE (ca. 1037-ca. 1157): In origin a dynasty of Turkish nomads from the steppes of Turkestan, the Seljuqs wrested Persia and Baghdad from the Buyids (q.v.) and at the height of their power in the late eleventh century controlled an empire stretching from Afghanistan to Syria.

ṬABARĪ (d. 923): Historian and Koranic commentator, Ṭabarī was the greatest exponent of the *Ḥadīth* school of historiography in classical Islam. A native of Ṭabaristān (south of the Caspian), Ṭabarī travelled widely but lived and taught in Baghdad. Apart from his universal history and his equally celebrated commentary on the Koran, Ṭabarī was a learned jurist, and his legal teachings were expounded for a while as a separate *madhhab* or legal "school." Only an excerpt of his history, covering the years 833-842, has been translated. See E. Marin, *The Reign of al-Muʾtaism* (New Haven, CT: American Oriental Society, 1951). A translation of the entire chronicle is in progress (1984) under the auspices of Columbia University.

TWELVER SHĪʿISM: Known also as Imāmī or Jaʿfarī Shīʿism, this has been the most numerous, though not always the most powerful, group within Shīʿism. It established its legal and doctrinal system between the mid-eighth and the late ninth centuries. Its focal point is loyalty to the traditions and teachings of the twelve *imāms* (ʿAlī, Ḥasan, Ḥusayn, Muḥammad, Jaʿfar, Mūsā, ʿAlī, Muḥammad, ʿAlī, Ḥasan, Muḥammad), descendants of the Prophet through his daughter Fāṭima and ʿAlī (q.v.), the first of the line. The last of the line, surnamed the "Mahdī," is absent, not dead, and his return will usher in a reign of justice and peace, and prepare for the world's end. Although Twelver legal thought is theoretically more liberal that Sunnite thought, historically speaking neither branch can be said to have been more liberal than the other. The differences in ritual, inheritance laws, and marriage contracts are in theory minor but they have had important socioeconomic consequences in certain Islamic countries at certain times.

UMAYYADS: Originally the most wealthy and powerful of Mecca's ruling families before and during Muḥammad's mission, the Umayyads were his determined enemies until shortly before his death, when they embraced Islam. They quickly surrounded Muḥammad and his first three caliphs as advisors, generals, and administrators of the new empire, and in 661 their chief, Muʿāwiya (q.v.), won control of the state from his base in Damascus. The Umayyads ruled until 750 and, under them, the administrative structure of the Arab Muslim state was delineated, but their cultural achievements are still inadequately known to modern scholarship.

ʿUTHMĀN (d. 655): The third caliph, Uthmān was a member of the Umayyad (q.v.) family. His accession signalled a crucial stage in the family's rise to supreme power. ʿUthmān was pious but weak, and his assassination by a group of disgruntled rebels marked the beginning of the first civil war *(fitna)* in Arab Islamic history. In Islamic tradition he is known as the first collector of the text of the Koran.

INDEX

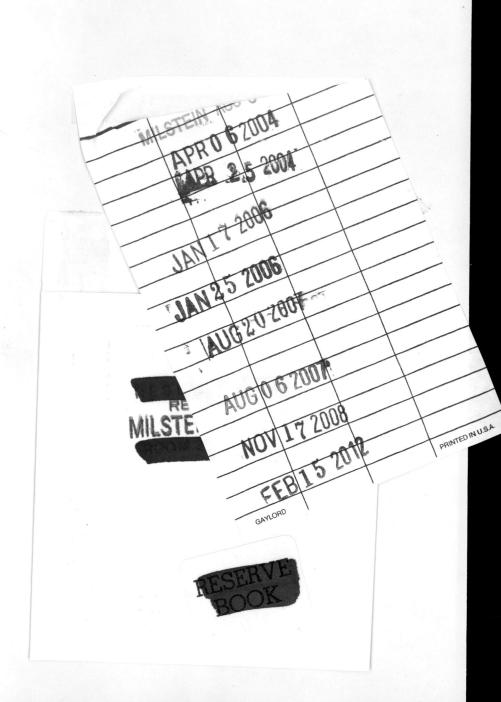